Non-L
Football
Supporters'
Guide
& Yearbook
2011

EDITOR
John Robinson

Nineteenth Edition

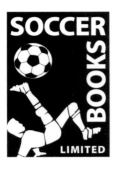

For details of our range of over 1,700 books and 350 DVDs, visit our web site or contact us using the information shown below.

British Library Cataloguing in Publication Data
A catalogue record for this book is available from the British Library

ISBN: 978-1-86223-198-6

Manufactured in the UK by LPPS Ltd, Wellingborough, NN8 3PJ

FOREWORD

Our thanks go to the numerous club officials who have aided us in the compilation of information contained in this guide and also to Michael Robinson (page layouts), Bob Budd (cover artwork) and Tony Brown (Cup Statistics – www.soccerdata.com) and Derek Mead for providing some of the photographs.

Where we use the term 'Child' for concessionary prices, this is often also the price charged to Senior Citizens. As the VAT rate will increase in 2011, supporters' should note that this will inevitably result in higher matchday admission prices compared to those shown.

The fixtures listed later in this book were released just a short time before we went to print and, as such, some of the dates shown may be subject to change. We therefore suggest that readers treat these fixtures as a rough guide and check dates carefully before attending matches.

Finally, we would like to wish our readers a safe and happy spectating season.

John Robinson
EDITOR

CONTENTS

THE FOOTBALL CONFERENCE BLUE SQUARE PREMIER

Address   Third Floor, Wellington House, 31-34 Waterloo Street, Birmingham   B2 5TJ

Phone (0121) 214-1950

Web site   www.footballconference.co.uk

Clubs for the 2010/2011 Season

AFC WIMBLEDON

Founded: 2002
Former Names: Originally formed as Wimbledon Old Centrals (1889-1905) who later became Wimbledon FC
Nickname: 'The Dons'
Ground: The Cherry Red Records Fans' Stadium – Kingsmeadow, Jack Goodchild Way, 422A Kingston Road, Kingston-upon-Thames, Surrey KT1 3PB
Record Attendance: 4,722 (2009)

Pitch Size: 115 × 80 yards
Ground Capacity: 4,700
Seating Capacity: 1,277
Colours: Shirts and Shorts are Blue with Yellow trim
Telephone Nº: (020) 8547-3528
Fax Number: 0808 280-0816
Web site: www.afcwimbledon.co.uk

GENERAL INFORMATION
Car Parking: At the ground
Coach Parking: At the ground
Nearest Railway Station: Norbiton (1 mile)
Nearest Bus Station: Kingston
Club Shop: At the ground
Opening Times: Matchdays only
Telephone Nº: (020) 8547-3528
Police Telephone Nº: (020) 8541-1212

GROUND INFORMATION
Away Supporters' Entrances & Sections:
No usual segregation

ADMISSION INFO (2010/2011 PRICES)
Adult Standing: £14.00
Adult Seating: £16.00 – £18.00
Concessionary Standing: £7.00
Concessionary Seating: £8.00 – £9.00
Under-16s Standing: £2.00
Under-16s Seating: £4.00 – £5.00
Programme Price: £2.50

DISABLED INFORMATION
Wheelchairs: Accommodated around the ground
Helpers: Please phone the club for information
Prices: Please phone the club for information
Disabled Toilets: Yes
Contact: (020) 8547-3528   (Bookings are necessary)

Travelling Supporters' Information:
Routes: Exit the M25 at Junction 10 and take the A3 to the New Malden/Worcester Park turn-off and turn into Malden Road (A2043). Follow Malden Road to the mini-roundabout and turn left into Kingston Road. Kingsmeadow is situated approximately 1 mile up the Kingston Road, on the left-hand side and is signposted from the mini-roundabout.

ALTRINCHAM FC

Founded: 1891
Former Names: Broadheath FC
Nickname: 'The Robins'
Ground: Moss Lane, Altrincham WA15 8AP
Record Attendance: 10,275 (February 1925)
Pitch Size: 110 × 72 yards

Colours: Red and White striped shirts, Black shorts
Telephone N°: (0161) 928-1045
Daytime Phone N°: (0161) 928-1045
Fax Number: (0161) 926-9934
Ground Capacity: 6,085
Seating Capacity: 1,154
Web site: www.altrinchamfc.com

GENERAL INFORMATION

Supporters Association: Brian Flynn, c/o Club
Telephone N°: 07860 561011
Car Parking: Limited street parking
Coach Parking: By Police Direction
Nearest Railway Station: Altrincham (5 minutes walk)
Nearest Bus Station: Altrincham
Club Shop: Inside the ground
Opening Times: Matchdays only. Opens one hour prior to the start of the game.
Telephone N°: (0161) 928-1045
Police Telephone N°: (0161) 872-5050

GROUND INFORMATION

Away Supporters' Entrances & Sections:
Hale End turnstiles and accommodation

ADMISSION INFO (2010/2011 PRICES)

Adult Standing: £13.00
Adult Seating: £15.00
Concessionary Standing: £8.00
Concessionary Seating: £9.00
Ages 12-16 years Standing/Seating: £5.00
Under-12s Standing/Seating: £2.00
Programme Price: £2.00

DISABLED INFORMATION

Wheelchairs: 3 spaces are available each for home and away fans adjacent to the Away dugout
Helpers: Admitted
Prices: Free for the disabled. £12.00 for helpers
Disabled Toilets: Yes
Contact: (0161) 928-1045 (Bookings are necessary)

Travelling Supporters' Information:
Routes: Exit the M56 at either Junction 6 or 7 and following the signs Altrincham FC.

BARROW FC

Founded: 1901
Former Names: None
Nickname: 'Bluebirds'
Ground: Holker Street Stadium, Barrow-in-Furness, Cumbria   LA14 5UW
Record Attendance: 16,874 (1954)
Pitch Size: 110 × 75 yards

Colours: White shirts with Blue shorts
Telephone Nº: (01229) 823061
Fax Number: (01229) 823061
Ground Capacity: 4,057
Seating Capacity: 928
Web site: www.barrowafc.com

GENERAL INFORMATION

Supporters Club: Bill Ablitt, c/o Club
Telephone Nº: (01229) 471617
Car Parking: Street Parking, Popular Side Car Park and Soccer Bar Car Park
Coach Parking: Adjacent to the ground
Nearest Railway Station: Barrow Central (½ mile)
Nearest Bus Station: ½ mile
Club Shop: At the ground
Opening Times: Monday to Friday 9.00am – 3.30pm and Saturdays 10.00am – 2.00pm
Telephone Nº: (01229) 823061
Police Telephone Nº: (01229) 824532

GROUND INFORMATION

Away Supporters' Entrances & Sections:
West Terrace (not covered)

ADMISSION INFO (2010/2011 PRICES)

Adult Standing: £13.00
Adult Seating: £14.00
Concessionary Standing: £10.00
Concessionary Seating: £11.00
Under-16s Standing/Seating: £5.00
Programme Price: £2.00

DISABLED INFORMATION

Wheelchairs: 6 spaces available in the Disabled Area
Helpers: Admitted
Prices: Normal prices apply
Disabled Toilets: Available
Contact: (01229) 823061   (Bookings are not necessary)

Travelling Supporters' Information:
Routes: Exit the M6 at Junction 36 and take the A590 through Ulverston. Using the bypass, follow signs for Barrow. After approximately 5 miles, turn left into Wilkie Road and the ground is on the right.

BATH CITY FC

Founded: 1889
Former Names: Bath AFC, Bath Railway FC and Bath Amateurs FC
Nickname: 'The Romans'
Ground: Twerton Park, Bath   BA2 1DB
Record Attendance: 18,020 (1960)
Pitch Size: 110 × 76 yards

Colours: Black and White striped shirts, Black shorts
Telephone Nº: (01225) 423087/313247
Fax Number: (01225) 481391
Ground Capacity: 8,840
Seating Capacity: 1,026
Web site: www.bathcityfc.com

GENERAL INFORMATION

Supporters Club: Martin Brush, c/o Club
Telephone Nº: (01225) 423087
Car Parking: 150 spaces available at the ground
Coach Parking: Available at the ground
Nearest Railway Station: Bath Spa (1½ miles)
Nearest Bus Station: Avon Street, Bath
Club Shop: Yes – contact Martin Brush, c/o Club
Opening Times: Matchdays and office hours
Telephone Nº: (01225) 423087

GROUND INFORMATION

Away Supporters' Entrances & Sections:
No usual segregation

ADMISSION INFO (2010/2011 PRICES)

Adult Standing: £13.00
Adult Seating: £14.00
Senior Citizen Standing: £9.00
Senior Citizen Seating: £10.00
Under-16s Standing: £4.00
Under-16s Seating: £5.00
Programme Price: £2.50

DISABLED INFORMATION

Wheelchairs: 10 spaces available each for home and away fans in front of the Family Stand
Helpers: Admitted
Prices: £9.00 for the disabled. Free entrance for helpers
Disabled Toilets: Available behind the Family Stand
Contact: (01225) 423087   (Bookings are not necessary)

Travelling Supporters' Information:
Route: As a recommendation, avoid exiting the M4 at Junction 18 as the road from takes you through Bath City Centre. Instead, exit the M4 at Junction 19 onto the M32. Turn off the M32 at Junction 1 and follow the A4174 Bristol Ring Road south then join the A4 for Bath. On the A4, after passing through Saltford you will reach a roundabout shortly before entering Bath. Take the 2nd exit at this roundabout then follow the road before turning left into Newton Road at the bottom of the steep hill. The ground is then on the right hand side of the road.

CAMBRIDGE UNITED FC

Founded: 1912
Former Name: Abbey United FC (1912-1951)
Nickname: 'U's' 'United'
Ground: The R Costings Abbey Stadium, Newmarket Road, Cambridge   CB5 8LN
Ground Capacity: 8,339
Seating Capacity: 4,376

Pitch Size: 110 × 74 yards
Record Attendance: 14,000 (1st May 1970)
Colours: Amber shirts, Black shorts
Telephone Nº: (01223) 566500
Ticket Office: (01223) 566500
Fax Number: (01223) 729220
Web Site: www.cambridgeunited.com

GENERAL INFORMATION

Car Parking: Street parking only
Coach Parking: Coldhams Road
Nearest Railway Station: Cambridge (2 miles)
Nearest Bus Station: Cambridge City Centre
Club Shop: At the ground
Opening Times: Monday to Friday 9.00am to 5.00pm and Matchdays 11.00am to kick-off
Telephone Nº: (01223) 566500
Police Telephone Nº: (01223) 358966

GROUND INFORMATION

Away Supporters' Entrances & Sections:
Coldham Common turnstiles 20-22 – Habbin Terrace (South) and South Stand (Seating) turnstiles 23-26

ADMISSION INFO (2010/2011 PRICES)

Adult Standing: £14.00
Adult Seating: £16.00 – £17.00
Child Standing: £5.00
Child Seating: £5.00 (in the Family Stand) or £5.00–£8.00
Concessionary Standing: £10.00
Concessionary Seating: £11.00 – £12.00
Programme Price: £3.00

DISABLED INFORMATION

Wheelchairs: 19 spaces in total for Home fans in the disabled sections, in front of Main Stand and in the North Terrace. 16 spaces for Away fans in the South Stand.
Helpers: One helper admitted per disabled fan
Prices: £9.00 for the disabled. Free of charge for helpers
Disabled Toilets: At the rear of the disabled section
Contact: (01223) 566500   (Bookings are necessary)

Travelling Supporters' Information: From the North: Take the A14 from Huntingdon, then turn east along the A14 dual carriageway. Exit the A14 at the 4th junction (to the east of Cambridge), up the slip road signposted Stow-cum-Quy then turn right onto the A1303, returning westwards towards Cambridge. Go straight on at the first roundabout passing the Airport on the left then straight on at two sets of traffic lights. Go straight on at the next roundabout and the ground is on the left after 700 yards; From the South: Exit the M11 at Junction 14 and turn east along the A14 dual carriageway. Then as from the North.
Bus Services: Services from the Railway Station to the City Centre and Nº 3 from the City Centre to the Ground.

CRAWLEY TOWN FC

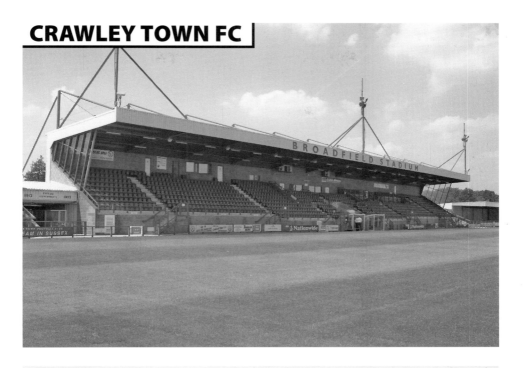

Founded: 1896
Former Names: None
Nickname: 'Red Devils'
Ground: Broadfield Stadium, Brighton Road, Crawley, Sussex RH11 9RX
Record Attendance: 4,516 (2004)
Pitch Size: 110 × 72 yards

Colours: Red shirts and shorts
Telephone Nº: (01293) 410000 (Ground)
Daytime Nº: (01293) 410000 (10.00am – 4.00pm)
Fax Number: (01293) 410002
Ground Capacity: 4,941
Seating Capacity: 1,150
Web site: www.crawleytownfc.net

GENERAL INFORMATION

Supporters Club: Alain Harper, 33 Nuthurst Close, Ifield, Crawley, Sussex
Telephone Nº: (01293) 511764
Car Parking: 350 spaces available at the ground
Coach Parking: At the ground
Nearest Railway Station: Crawley (1 mile)
Nearest Bus Station: By the Railway Station
Club Shop: At the ground
Opening Times: Weekdays 10.00am to 4.00pm; Saturday matches 12.00pm to kick-off then one hour after the game; Mid-week matches 6.00pm to kick-off then one hour after the game
Telephone Nº: (01293) 410000
Police Telephone Nº: (08456) 070999

GROUND INFORMATION

Away Supporters' Entrances & Sections:
No usual segregation

ADMISSION INFO (2010/2011 PRICES)

Adult Standing: £14.00
Adult Seating: £17.00 (£40.00 in the Executive Area)
Child Standing: £5.00 (Under-7s admitted free of charge)
Child Seating: £6.00 (Under-7s admitted free of charge)
Senior Citizen/Student Standing: £11.00
Senior Citizen/Student Seating: £13.00
Programme Price: £2.50

DISABLED INFORMATION

Wheelchairs: Accommodated in the disabled section of the Main Stand (Lift access available)
Helpers: One helper admitted per disabled fan
Prices: Normal prices apply
Disabled Toilets: Available
Contact: (01293) 410000 (Bookings are not necessary)

Travelling Supporters' Information:
Routes: Exit the M23 at Junction 11 and take the A23 towards Crawley. After ¼ mile, the Stadium is on the left. Take the first exit at the roundabout for the Stadium entrance.

DARLINGTON FC

Founded: 1883
Nickname: 'Quakers'
Ground: Darlington Arena, Hurworth Moor, Neasham Road, Darlington DL2 1DL
Ground Capacity: 25,321 (All seats)
Record Attendance: 10,224 (16th August 2003)
Pitch Size: 115 × 74 yards

Colours: White and Black shirts with White shorts
Telephone Nº: (01325) 387000
Ticket Office: 0871 855-1883
Fax Number: (01325) 387050
Web Site: www.darlington-fc.net

GENERAL INFORMATION

Car Parking: Limited number of spaces at the ground
Coach Parking: At the ground
Nearest Railway Station: Darlington (1½ miles)
Nearest Bus Station: Darlington Central
Club Shop: At the ground
Opening Times: Monday to Friday 10.00am – 5.00pm and Saturday matchdays 10.00am – 3.00pm
Telephone Nº: (01325) 387020
Police Telephone Nº: (01325) 467681

GROUND INFORMATION

Away Supporters' Entrances & Sections:
East Stand

ADMISSION INFO (2010/2011 PRICES)

Adult Seating: £16.00 (Matchday price £18.00)
Senior Citizen/Student Seating: £10.00 (Matchday £12)
Under-16s Seating: £5.00
Note: Price reductions are available if tickets are pre-booked
Programme Price: £2.50

DISABLED INFORMATION

Wheelchairs: Spaces available in disabled sections throughout the ground. Lifts are available in the stands
Helpers: One helper admitted per disabled person
Prices: £10.00 for the disabled and blind (£12.00 if purchased on the Matchday). Free of charge for helpers
Disabled Toilets: Available in all stands
Contact: (01325) 387000

Travelling Supporters' Information:
Routes: From All Parts: Take the A1 to the A66(M) and follow the road to it's end. Take the 1st exit at the roundabout, go up the hill then, at the second roundabout, take the 3rd exit signposted A66 Teeside. The ground is at the next roundabout after approximately 1 mile.

EASTBOURNE BOROUGH FC

Founded: 1963
Former Names: Langney Sports FC
Nickname: 'The Sports'
Ground: Langney Sports Club, Priory Lane,
Eastbourne   BN23 7QH
Record Attendance: 3,770 (5th November 2005)
Pitch Size: 115 × 72 yards

Colours: Red shirts with Black shorts
Telephone Nº: (01323) 766265
Fax Number: (01323) 741627
Ground Capacity: 4,100
Seating Capacity: 542
Web site: www.ebfc.co.uk

GENERAL INFORMATION

Supporters Club: Yes – c/o Club
Telephone Nº: (01323) 766265
Car Parking: Around 400 spaces available at the ground
Coach Parking: At the ground
Nearest Railway Station: Pevensey & Westham (1½ miles but no public transport to the ground)
Nearest Bus Station: Eastbourne   (Service 6A to ground)
Club Shop: At the ground
Opening Times: Wednesday to Friday 11.00am to 1.00pm and Matchdays
Telephone Nº: (01323) 766265
Police Telephone Nº: (0845) 607-0999

GROUND INFORMATION

Away Supporters' Entrances & Sections:
No usual segregation

ADMISSION INFO (2010/2011 PRICES)

Adult Standing: £14.00
Adult Seating: £16.00
Under-16s Standing: £4.00
Under-16s Seating: £6.00
Senior Citizen Standing: £10.00
Senior Citizen Seating: £12.00
Programme Price: £2.50

DISABLED INFORMATION

Wheelchairs: 6 spaces available
Helpers: Admitted
Prices: Normal prices apply
Disabled Toilets: Available
Contact: (01323) 766265   (Bookings are necessary)

Travelling Supporters' Information:
Routes: From the North: Exit the A22 onto the Polegate bypass, signposted A27 Eastbourne, Hastings & Bexhill. *Take the 2nd exit at the next roundabout for Stone Cross and Westham (A22) then the first exit at the following roundabout signposted Stone Cross and Westham. Turn right after ½ mile into Friday Street (B2104). At the end of Friday Street, turn left at the double mini-roundabout into Hide Hollow (B2191), passing Eastbourne Crematorium on your right. Turn right at the roundabout into Priory Road, and Priory Lane is about 200 yards down the road on the left; Approaching on the A27 from Brighton: Turn left at the Polegate traffic lights then take 2nd exit at the large roundabout to join the bypass. Then as from *.

FLEETWOOD TOWN FC

Founded: 1977
Former Names: None (The club succeeded Fleetwood FC who existed from 1907-1977)
Nickname: 'The Fishermen'
Ground: Highbury Stadium, Park Avenue, Fleetwood   FY7 6TX
Record Attendance: 6,150 vs Rochdale FC (1965)

Pitch Size: 112 × 71 yards
Colours: Red shirts with White sleeves, White shorts
Telephone N°: (01253) 770702
Fax Number: (01253) 770702
Ground Capacity: 3,450
Seating Capacity: 550
Web site: www.fleetwoodtownfc.com

GENERAL INFORMATION

Car Parking: Spaces for 40 cars at the ground and also street parking
Coach Parking: At the ground
Nearest Railway Station: Poulton (7 miles)
Nearest Bus Station: Fleetwood
Club Shop: Sales via the club web site only
Opening Times: –
Telephone N°: –

GROUND INFORMATION

Away Supporters' Entrances & Sections:
No usual segregation

ADMISSION INFO (2010/2011 PRICES)

Adult Standing: £12.50
Adult Seating: £12.50
Child Standing: £7.00
Child Seating: £7.00
Senior Citizen Standing: £8.00
Senior Citizen Seating: £8.00
Programme Price: £2.50

DISABLED INFORMATION

Wheelchairs: Accommodated
Helpers: Admitted
Prices: Normal prices apply for the disabled and helpers
Disabled Toilets: Available
Contact: (01253) 770702   (Bookings are necessary)

Travelling Supporters' Information:
Routes: Exit the M55 at Junction 3 and take the A585 to Fleetwood (approximately 11½ miles). Upon reaching Fleetwood, take the 1st exit at the Nautical College roundabout (with the statue of Eros in the middle) and continue for about 1 mile to the next roundabout. Take the 6th exit onto Hatfield Avenue and after about ½ mile (when the road bends to the right)m turn left into Nelson Road. The ground is situated on the left after 100 yards.

FOREST GREEN ROVERS FC

Founded: 1889
Former Names: Stroud FC
Nickname: 'The Rovers'
Ground: The New Lawn, Smiths Way,
Forest Green, Nailsworth, Gloucestershire, GL6 0FG
Record Attendance: 4,836 (3rd January 2009)
Pitch Size: 110 × 70 yards

Colours: Black and White striped shirts, Black shorts
Telephone Nº: (01453) 834860
Fax Number: (01453) 835291
Ground Capacity: 5,147
Seating Capacity: 2,500
Web site: www.forestgreenroversfc.com

GENERAL INFORMATION
Supporters Club: Sam Read, c/o Club
Telephone Nº: (01453) 834860
Car Parking: At the ground
Coach Parking: At the ground
Nearest Railway Station: Stroud (4 miles)
Nearest Bus Station: Nailsworth
Club Shop: At the ground
Opening Times: Matchdays only
Telephone Nº: (01453) 834860
Police Telephone Nº: 0845 090-1234

GROUND INFORMATION
Away Supporters' Entrances & Sections:
South Stand

ADMISSION INFO (2010/2011 PRICES)
Adult Standing: £13.00
Adult Seating: £15.00
Senior Citizen Standing: £8.00
Senior Citizen Seating: £10.00
Child Standing: £5.00
Child Seating: £7.00
Programme Price: £2.50

DISABLED INFORMATION
Wheelchairs: Accommodated in the Main Stand
Helpers: Admitted
Prices: Normal prices for the disabled. Free for helpers
Disabled Toilets: Yes
Contact: (01453) 834860   (Enquiries necessary at least 72 hours in advance)

Travelling Supporters' Information:
Routes: The ground is located 4 miles south of Stroud on the A46 to Bath. Upon entering Nailsworth, turn into Spring Hill at the mini-roundabout and the ground is approximately ½ mile up the hill on the left.

GATESHEAD FC

Founded: 1930   (Reformed in 1977)
Former Names: Gateshead United FC
Nickname: 'Tynesiders'
Ground: International Stadium, Neilson Road,
Gateshead   NE10 0EF
Record Attendance: 11,750 (1995)
Pitch Size: 110 × 70 yards

Colours: White shirts with Black shorts
Telephone Nº: (0191) 478-3883
Daytime Phone Nº: (0191) 373-7014
Fax Number: (0191) 440-0404
Ground Capacity: 11,750
Seating Capacity: 11,750
Web site: www.gateshead-fc.com

GENERAL INFORMATION
Supporters Club: c/o Club
Telephone Nº: –
Car Parking: At the stadium
Coach Parking: At the stadium
Nearest Railway Station: Gateshead Stadium Metro
(½ mile); Newcastle (British Rail) 1½ miles
Nearest Bus Station: Heworth Interchange (½ mile)
Club Shop: At the stadium
Opening Times: Matchdays only
Telephone Nº: (0191) 478-3883
Police Telephone Nº: (0191) 232-3451

GROUND INFORMATION
Away Supporters' Entrances & Sections:
Tyne & Wear County Stand North End

ADMISSION INFO (2010/2011 PRICES)
Adult Seating: £13.00
Senior Citizen/Concessionary Seating: £8.00
Under-16s Seating: Free if accompanying a paying adult
Programme Price: £2.50

DISABLED INFORMATION
Wheelchairs: 5 spaces available each for home and away
fans by the trackside – Level access with automatic doors
Helpers: Please phone the club for information
Prices: Please phone the club for information
Disabled Toilets: Available in the Reception Area and on
the 1st floor concourse – accessible by lift.
Contact: (0191) 478-3883   (Bookings are necessary)

Travelling Supporters' Information:
Routes: From the South: Take the A1(M) to Washington Services and fork right onto the A194(M) signposted Tyne Tunnel. At
the next roundabout, turn left onto the A184 signposted for Gateshead. The Stadium is on the right after 3 miles.

GRIMSBY TOWN FC

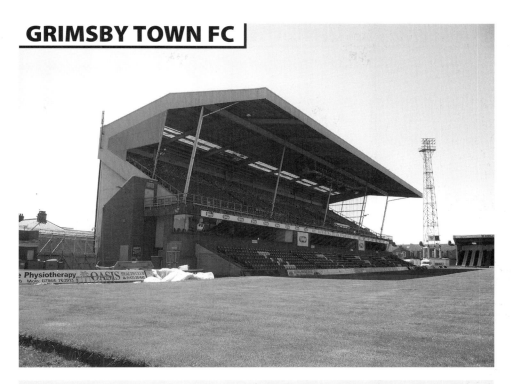

Founded: 1878
Former Names: Grimsby Pelham FC (1879)
Nickname: 'Mariners'
Ground: Blundell Park, Cleethorpes   DN35 7PY
Ground Capacity: 8,974 (All seats)
Record Attendance: 31,651 (20th February 1937)
Pitch Size: 111 × 74 yards

Colours: Black and White striped shirts, Black shorts
Telephone Nº: (01472) 605050
Ticket Office: (01472) 605050
Fax Number: (01472) 693665
Web Site: www.gtfc.co.uk

GENERAL INFORMATION

Car Parking: Street parking
Coach Parking: Harrington Street – near the ground
Nearest Railway Station: Cleethorpes (1½ miles)
Nearest Bus Station: Brighowgate, Grimsby (4 miles)
Club Shop: At the ground
Opening Times: Monday – Friday 9.00am to 5.00pm; Matchday Saturdays 9.00am to kick-off
Telephone Nº: (01472) 605050
Police Telephone Nº: (01472) 359171

GROUND INFORMATION

Away Supporters' Entrances & Sections:
Harrington Street turnstiles 15-18 and Constitution Avenue turnstiles 5-14

ADMISSION INFO (2010/2011 PRICES)

Adult Seating: £18.00 (Away fans £18.00)
Senior Citizens/Young Adults (Ages 15–18): £12.00
Child Seating: £8.00 (Under-15s)
Programme Price: £2.50

DISABLED INFORMATION

Wheelchairs: 50 spaces in total for Home and Away fans in the disabled section, in front of the Main Stand
Helpers: Helpers are admitted
Prices: £18.00 for the disabled. Free of charge for helpers
Disabled Toilets: Available in disabled section
Commentaries are available in disabled section
Contact: (01472) 605050   (Bookings are necessary)

Travelling Supporters' Information:
Routes: From All Parts except Lincolnshire and East Anglia: Take the M180 to the A180 and follow signs for Grimsby/Cleethorpes. The A180 ends at a roundabout (the 3rd in short distance after crossing docks), take the 2nd exit from the roundabout over the Railway flyover into Cleethorpes Road (A1098) and continue into Grimsby Road. After the second stretch of dual carriageway, the ground is ½ mile on the left; From Lincolnshire: Take the A46 or A16 and follow Cleethorpes signs along (A1098) Weelsby Road for 2 miles. Take the 1st exit at the roundabout at the end of Clee Road into Grimsby Road. The ground is 1¾ miles on the right.

HAYES & YEADING UNITED FC

Founded: 2007
Former Names: Formed by the amalgamation of Hayes FC and Yeading FC in 2007
Nickname: 'United'
Ground: Church Road, Hayes, Middlesex UB3 2LE
Record Attendance: 15,370 (10th February 1951)
Pitch Size: 117 × 70 yards

Colours: Red shirts with Black shorts
Telephone Nº: (020) 8573-2075
Fax Number: (020) 8573-0933
Ground Capacity: 4,300
Seating Capacity: 500
Web site: www.hyufc.net

GENERAL INFORMATION

Supporters Club: Lee Hermitage, c/o Hayes & Yeading United FC
Telephone Nº: (020) 8573-2075
Car Parking: 300 spaces available at the ground
Coach Parking: By arrangement
Nearest Railway Station: Hayes & Harlington (1 mile)
Nearest Bus Station: Hayes
Club Shop: At the ground
Opening Times: Matchdays only. Saturday matches from 2.00pm–5.00pm. Weekday matches from 6.45pm–9.30pm
Telephone Nº: (020) 8573-2075
Police Telephone Nº: (020) 8900-7212

GROUND INFORMATION

Away Supporters' Entrances & Sections:
Church Road End when segregated (not usual)

ADMISSION INFO (2010/2011 PRICES)

Adult Standing: £14.00
Adult Seating: £16.00
Child/Senior Citizen Standing: £8.00
Child/Senior Citizen Seating: £10.00
Programme Price: £2.00

DISABLED INFORMATION

Wheelchairs: Accommodated as necessary
Helpers: Admitted
Prices: £14.00 for the disabled but a helper is admitted free of charge with each paying disabled fan
Disabled Toilets: Available
Contact: (020) 8573-2075   (Bookings are not necessary)

Travelling Supporters' Information:
Routes: From the A40: Approaching London, take the Ruislip junction – turn right onto the B455 Ruislip Road to the White Hart Roundabout. Take the Hayes bypass to Uxbridge Road (A4020), turn right, then Church Road is ¾ mile on the left, opposite the Adam & Eve pub; From the M4: Exit at Junction 3 and take the A312 to Parkway towards Southall, then the Hayes bypass to Uxbridge Road (A4020). Turn left, then as above.

HISTON FC

Founded: 1904
Former Names: Histon Institute FC
Nickname: 'The Stutes'
Ground: The Glass World Stadium, Bridge Road, Impington, Cambridge CB24 9PH
Record Attendance: 6,400 (1956)
Pitch Size: 110 × 75 yards

Colours: Red and Black striped shirts, Black shorts
Telephone Nº: (01223) 237373
Fax Number: (01223) 237373
Ground Capacity: 4,100
Seating Capacity: 1,626
Web site: www.histonfc.co.uk

GENERAL INFORMATION

Supporters Club: Yes
Telephone Nº: (01223) 846455 (Jenny Wells)
Car Parking: Permit holders and disabled parking only at the ground. Check web site for details of fans parking
Coach Parking: For team coaches only
Nearest Railway Station: Cambridge (4 miles)
Nearest Bus Station: Cambridge (4 miles) (Use Citi Seven service for the ground)
Club Shop: At the ground
Opening Times: Three hours prior to kick-off for both Saturday and evening matches.
Telephone Nº: (01223) 237373

GROUND INFORMATION

Away Supporters' Entrances & Sections:
No usual segregation

ADMISSION INFO (2010/2011 PRICES)

Adult Standing: £14.00
Adult Seating: £15.00
Child Standing: £3.00
Child Seating: £4.00
Senior Citizen Standing: £9.00
Senior Citizen Seating: £10.00
Programme Price: £2.50

DISABLED INFORMATION

Wheelchairs: 6 spaces available in the home section and 6 spaces available in the away section
Helpers: Admitted
Prices: Concessionary prices for disabled. Free for helpers
Disabled Toilets: Available in both the home and away sections
Contact: Mac McDonald (Club safety officer) 07730 557021

Travelling Supporters' Information:
Routes: Exit the M11 at Junction 14 and follow the A14 eastwards. Take the first exit onto the B1049 (signposted Histon & Cottenham). Turn left at the traffic lights at the top of the slip road and pass the Holiday Inn on the right. Continue over the bridge and the entrance to the ground is on the right.

KETTERING TOWN FC

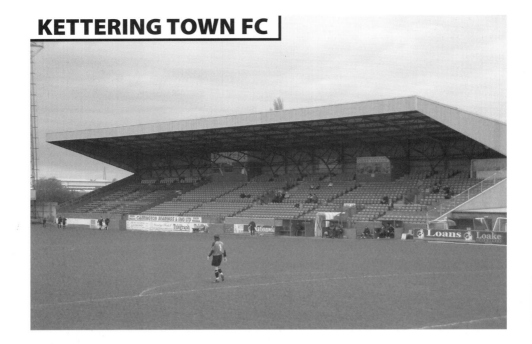

Founded: 1872
Former Names: Kettering FC
Nickname: 'The Poppies'
Ground: Elgood's Brewery Arena, Rockingham Road, Kettering, Northants NN16 9AW
Record Attendance: 11,526 (1947-48)
Pitch Size: 110 × 70 yards

Colours: Red shirts with Black shorts and socks
Telephone Nº: (01536) 483028
Daytime Phone Nº: (01536) 517013
Fax Number: (01536) 412273
Ground Capacity: Approximately 5,300
Seating Capacity: Approximately 1,550
Web site: www.ketteringtownfc.co.uk
E-mail: info@ketteringtownfc.co.uk

GENERAL INFORMATION
Supporters Club: c/o Club
Car Parking: At the ground
Coach Parking: As directed by the club
Nearest Railway Station: Kettering (1½ miles)
Nearest Bus Station: Kettering (1 mile)
Club Shop: At the ground
Opening Times: Matchdays only
Telephone Nº: (01536) 520035
Police Telephone Nº: (01536) 411411

GROUND INFORMATION
Away Supporters' Entrances & Sections:
Rockingham Road terrace and the Main Stand, Entrance A when applicable

ADMISSION INFO (2010/2011 PRICES)
Adult Standing: £10.00 (£12.00 for policed games)
Adult Seating: £10.00 (£12.00 for policed games)
Senior Citizen Standing: £10.00 (£12 for policed games)
Senior Citizen Seating: £10.00 (£12 for policed games)
Under-16s Standing: £1.00 (£2.00 for policed games)
Under-16s Seating: £1.00 (£2.00 for policed games)
Programme Price: £3.00

DISABLED INFORMATION
Wheelchairs: 7 spaces are available on the terracing adjacent to the Main Stand
Helpers: One helper admitted per wheelchair
Prices: Terrace prices for the disabled. Free for helpers
Disabled Toilets: Available
Contact: (01536) 483028 (Bookings are not necessary)

Travelling Supporters' Information:
Routes: To reach Kettering from the A1, M1 or M6, use the A14 to Junction 7, follow the A43 for 1 mile, turn right at the roundabout and the ground is 400 yards on the left on the A6003. (The ground is situated to the North of Kettering (1 mile) on the main A6003 Rockingham Road to Oakham).

KIDDERMINSTER HARRIERS FC

Founded: 1886
Nickname: 'Harriers'
Ground: Aggborough, Hoo Road, Kidderminster, Worcestershire DY10 1NB
Ground Capacity: 6,444
Seating Capacity: 3,143
Record Attendance: 9,155 (1948)

Pitch Size: 110 × 72 yards
Colours: Red shirts and shorts
Telephone Nº: (01562) 823931
Fax Number: (01562) 827329
Web Site: www.harriers.co.uk

GENERAL INFORMATION

Car Parking: At the ground
Coach Parking: As directed
Nearest Railway Station: Kidderminster
Nearest Bus Station: Kidderminster Town Centre
Club Shop: At the ground
Opening Times: Weekdays and First Team Matchdays 9.00am to 5.00pm
Telephone Nº: (01562) 823931
Police Telephone Nº: –

GROUND INFORMATION

Away Supporters' Entrances & Sections:
John Smiths Stand Entrance D and South Terrace Entrance E

ADMISSION INFO (2010/2011 PRICES)

Adult Standing: £14.00
Adult Seating: £17.00
Senior Citizen Standing: £8.00   **Under-16s:** £5.00
Senior Citizen Seating: £11.00   **Under-16s:** £8.00
Note: Under-8s are admitted free with a paying adult
Programme Price: £2.50

DISABLED INFORMATION

Wheelchairs: Home fans accommodated at the front of the Main Stand, Away fans in front of the John Smiths Stand
Helpers: Admitted
Prices: £10.00 for each disabled fan plus one helper
Disabled Toilets: Available by the disabled area
Contact: (01562) 823931   (Bookings are not necessary)

Travelling Supporters' Information:
Routes: Exit the M5 at Junction 3 and follow the A456 to Kidderminster. The ground is situated close by the Severn Valley Railway Station so follow the brown Steam Train signs and turn into Hoo Road about 200 yards downhill of the station. Follow the road along for ¼ mile and the ground is on the left.

LUTON TOWN FC

Founded: 1885
Former Names: The club was formed by the amalgamation of Wanderers FC and Excelsior FC
Nickname: 'Hatters'
Ground: Kenilworth Road Stadium, 1 Maple Road, Luton   LU4 8AW
Ground Capacity: 10,226 (All seats)
Record Attendance: 30,069 (4th March 1959)

Pitch Size: 110 × 72 yards
Colours: Shirts are White with Black trim, Black shorts
Telephone Nº: (01582) 411622
Ticket Office: (01582) 416976
Fax Number: (01582) 405070
Web Site: www.lutontown.co.uk

GENERAL INFORMATION
Car Parking: Street parking
Coach Parking: Luton Bus Station
Nearest Railway Station: Luton (1 mile)
Nearest Bus Station: Bute Street, Luton
Club Shop: Kenilworth Road Forecourt
Opening Times: 10.00am to 4.00pm
Telephone Nº: (01582) 411622
Police Telephone Nº: (01582) 401212

GROUND INFORMATION
Away Supporters' Entrances & Sections:
Oak Road for the Oak Stand

ADMISSION INFO (2010/2011 PRICES)
Adult Seating: £15.00 – £18.00
Under-10s Seating: £5.00
Under-17s Seating: £8.00
Under-22s Seating: £13.00
Senior Citizen Seating: £10.00 – £13.00
Note: Tickets are cheaper if bought prior to the matchday
Programme Price: £3.00

DISABLED INFORMATION
Wheelchairs: 32 spaces in total for Home and Away fans in the disabled section, Kenilworth Road End and Main Stand
Helpers: One helper admitted per disabled person
Prices: £15.00 for the disabled. Free of charge for helpers
Disabled Toilets: Available adjacent to disabled area
Commentaries are available for the blind
Contact: (01582) 416976   (Bookings are necessary)

Travelling Supporters' Information:
Routes: From the North and West: Exit the M1 at Junction 11 and follow signs for Luton (A505) into Dunstable Road. Follow the one-way system and turn right back towards Dunstable, take the second left into Ash Road for the ground; From the South and East: Exit the M1 at Junction 10 (or A6/A612) into Luton Town Centre and follow signs into Dunstable Road. After the railway bridge, take the sixth turning on the left into Ash Road for the ground.

MANSFIELD TOWN FC

Founded: 1897
Former Name: Mansfield Wesleyans FC (1897-1905)
Nickname: 'Stags'
Ground: Field Mill Ground, Quarry Lane, Mansfield, Nottinghamshire NG18 5DA
Ground Capacity: 10,000 (All seats)
Record Attendance: 24,467 (10th January 1953)
Pitch Size: 114 × 70 yards

Colours: Amber shirts with Royal Blue piping, Royal Blue shorts with Amber flash
Telephone Nº: (01623) 482483
Ticket Office: (01623) 482483
Fax Number: (01623) 482495
Web Site: www.mansfieldtown.net
E-mail: info@mansfieldtown.net

GENERAL INFORMATION

Car Parking: Large car park at the ground (£2.50)
Coach Parking: Adjacent to the ground
Nearest Railway Station: Mansfield (5 minutes walk)
Nearest Bus Station: Mansfield
Club Shop: In the South Stand of the Stadium
Opening Times: Weekdays 9.00am – 5.00pm and Matchdays 10.00am – 3.00pm
Telephone Nº: (0870) 756-3160
Police Telephone Nº: (01623) 420999

GROUND INFORMATION

Away Supporters' Entrances & Sections:
North Stand turnstiles for North Stand seating

ADMISSION INFO (2010/2011 PRICES)

Adult Seating: £15.00 – £18.00
Senior Citizen Seating: £12.00
Junior Seating: £7.00 – £9.00
Programme Price: £2.50

DISABLED INFORMATION

Wheelchairs: 90 spaces available in total in the disabled sections in the North Stand, Quarry Street Stand & West Stand
Helpers: Admitted
Prices: £8.00 for the disabled. Helpers £15.00
Disabled Toilets: Available in the North Stand, West Stand and Quarry Lane Stand
Contact: (0870) 756-3160 (Please buy tickets in advance)

Travelling Supporters' Information:
Routes: From the North: Exit the M1 at Junction 29 and take the A617 to Mansfield. After 6¼ miles turn right at the Leisure Centre into Rosemary Street. Carry on to Quarry Lane and turn right; From the South and West: Exit the M1 at Junction 28 and take the A38 to Mansfield. After 6½ miles turn right at the crossroads into Belvedere Street then turn right after ¼ mile into Quarry Lane; From the East: Take the A617 to Rainworth, turn left at the crossroads after 3 miles into Windsor Road and turn right at the end into Nottingham Road, then left into Quarry Lane.

NEWPORT COUNTY AFC

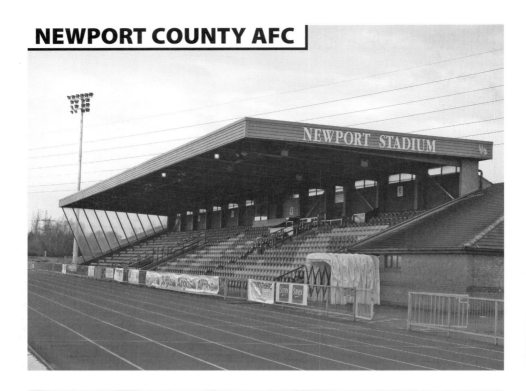

Founded: 1989
Former Names: Newport AFC
Nickname: 'The Exiles'
Ground: Newport Stadium, Stadium Way, Newport International Sports Village, Newport NP19 4PT
Record Attendance: 4,616 (11th November 2006)
Pitch Size: 112 × 72 yards

Colours: Amber shirts with Black shorts
Telephone Nº: (01633) 662262
Fax Number: (01633) 666107
Ground Capacity: 4,300
Seating Capacity: 1,236
Web site: www.newport-county.co.uk

GENERAL INFORMATION

Supporters Club: Bob Herrin, c/o Club
Telephone Nº: (01633) 274440
Car Parking: Space for 500 cars at the ground
Coach Parking: At the ground
Nearest Railway Station: Newport
Nearest Bus Station: Newport
Club Shop: At the ground
Opening Times: Matchdays only
Telephone Nº: (01633) 662262
Police Telephone Nº: (01633) 244999

GROUND INFORMATION

Away Supporters' Entrances & Sections:
No segregation unless specifically required by Police

ADMISSION INFO (2010/2011 PRICES)

Adult Standing: £13.00   **Adult Seating**: £14.00
Senior Citizen Standing: £9.00
Senior Citizen Seating: £10.00
Full-time Student Standing: £6.00
Full-time Student Seating: £8.00
Under-16s Standing: £3.00   **Under-16s Seating**: £5.00
Under-12s Seating: £3.00
Programme Price: £2.80

DISABLED INFORMATION

Wheelchairs: Accommodated
Helpers: Admitted
Prices: Normal prices for the disabled. Free for helpers
Disabled Toilets: Yes
Contact: (01633) 662262   (Bookings are not necessary)

Travelling Supporters' Information:
Routes: Exit the M4 at Junction 24 and take the A48 exit at the roundabout, signposted 'Newport Int. Sports Village'. Go straight on at the first two roundabouts then bear left at the 3rd roundabout. Carry straight on over the next two roundabouts, then turn left before the Carcraft site. Take the 1st turning on the left into the Stadium car park.

RUSHDEN & DIAMONDS FC

Founded: 1992
Former Names: Formed by the amalgamation of Rushden Town FC and Irthlingborough Diamonds FC
Nickname: 'Diamonds'
Ground: Nene Park, Diamond Way, Irthlingborough, Northants NN9 5QF
Ground Capacity: 6,441
Seating Capacity: 4,641

Record Attendance: 6,431 (vs Leeds United in 1999)
Pitch Size: 111 × 74 yards
Colours: Shirts, shorts and socks are White with Blue and Red trim
Telephone Nº: (01933) 652000
Ticket Office Nº: (01933) 652936
Fax Number: (01933) 654190
Web Site: www.thediamondsfc.com

GENERAL INFORMATION
Car Parking: At the ground (£3.00 charge)
Coach Parking: At the ground (£10.00 charge)
Nearest Railway Station: Wellingborough (5 miles)
Nearest Bus Station: Wellingborough
Club Shop: Yes – at the front of the Stadium
Opening Times: Weekdays 10.00am to 5.00pm; Matchdays 10.00am until kick-off then 30 minutes after the game.
Telephone Nº: (01933) 652000
Police Telephone Nº: (01933) 440333

GROUND INFORMATION
Away Supporters' Entrances & Sections:
Large following: Airwair Stand – enter via gates T/S/R
Smaller following: South Stand Block C5 – gates K/L

ADMISSION INFO (2009/2010 PRICES)
Adult Standing: £13.00 (Home fans only)
Adult Seating: £16.00
Concessionary Standing: £8.00
Concessionary Seating: £11.00
Under-16s Standing/Seating: £5.00
Note: Under-8s are admitted free with a paying adult
Programme Price: £3.00

DISABLED INFORMATION
Wheelchairs: Accommodated around the ground
Helpers: Admitted
Prices: £8.00 or £11.00 for the disabled fans with registered carers admitted free of charge
Disabled Toilets: Available around the ground
Contact: (01933) 652936 Matt Banyard

Travelling Supporters' Information:
Routes: The ground is located on the A6 about 350 yards north of the junction with the A45 (over the bridge). This is approximately 6 miles south of the A14.

SOUTHPORT FC

Founded: 1881
Former Names: Southport Vulcan FC, Southport Central FC
Nickname: 'The Sandgrounders'
Ground: Haig Avenue, Southport, Merseyside, PR8 6JZ
Record Attendance: 20,010 (1932)
Pitch Size: 110 × 77 yards

Colours: Yellow shirts and shorts
Telephone Nº: (01704) 533422
Fax Number: (01704) 533455
Ground Capacity: 6,001
Seating Capacity: 1,640
Web site: www.southportfc.net

GENERAL INFORMATION

Supporters Club: Grandstand Club
Telephone Nº: (01704) 530182
Car Parking: Street parking
Coach Parking: Adjacent to the ground
Nearest Railway Station: Southport (1½ miles)
Nearest Bus Station: Southport Town Centre
Club Shop: At the ground
Opening Times: Matchdays from 1.30pm (from 6.30pm on evening matchdays)
Telephone Nº: (01704) 533422
Police Telephone Nº: (0151) 709-6010

GROUND INFORMATION

Away Supporters' Entrances & Sections:
Blowick End entrances

ADMISSION INFO (2010/2011 PRICES)

Adult Standing: £12.50
Adult Seating: £14.00
Child/Senior Citizen Standing: £9.00
Child/Senior Citizen Seating: £10.00
Programme Price: £2.50

DISABLED INFORMATION

Wheelchairs: Accommodated in front of the Grandstand
Helpers: Admitted
Prices: Concessionary prices charged for the disabled. Helpers are admitted free of charge
Disabled Toilets: Available at the Blowick End of the Grandstand
Contact: (01704) 533422   (Bookings are not necessary)

Travelling Supporters' Information:
Routes: Exit the M58 at Junction 3 and take the A570 to Southport. At the major roundabout (McDonalds/Tesco) go straight on into Scarisbrick New Road, pass over the brook and turn right into Haig Avenue at the traffic lights. The ground is then on the right-hand side.

TAMWORTH FC

Founded: 1933
Former Names: None
Nickname: 'The Lambs'
Ground: The Lamb Ground, Kettlebrook, Tamworth, B77 1AA
Record Attendance: 4,920 (3rd April 1948)
Pitch Size: 110 × 73 yards

Colours: Red shirts and shorts
Telephone Nº: (01827) 65798
Fax Number: (01827) 62236
Ground Capacity: 4,118
Seating Capacity: 520
Web site: www.thelambs.co.uk

GENERAL INFORMATION

Supporters Club: Dave Clayton, c/o Club
Car Parking: 200 spaces available at the ground – £2.00 per car, £5.00 for per minibus or £10.00 per coach
Coach Parking: At the ground
Nearest Railway Station: Tamworth (½ mile)
Nearest Bus Station: Tamworth (½ mile)
Club Shop: At the ground
Opening Times: Weekdays & Matchdays 10.00am – 4.00pm
Telephone Nº: (01827) 65798
Police Telephone Nº: (01827) 61001

GROUND INFORMATION

Away Supporters' Entrances & Sections:
Gates 1 and 2 for Terracing, Gate 2A for seating

ADMISSION INFO (2010/2011 PRICES)

Adult Standing: £10.00 – £14.00
Adult Seating: £12.00 – £16.00
Child/Senior Citizen Standing: £5.00 – £9.00
Child/Senior Citizen Seating: £5.00 – £9.00
Note: Prices vary depending on the category of the game
Programme Price: £2.50

DISABLED INFORMATION

Wheelchairs: Accommodated
Helpers: Admitted
Prices: Normal prices apply for Wheelchair disabled. Helpers are charged concessionary rates
Disabled Toilets: Yes
Contact: (01827) 65798 (Bookings are advisable)

Travelling Supporters' Information:
Routes: Exit the M42 at Junction 10 and take the A5/A51 to the town centre following signs for Town Centre/Snowdome. The follow signs for Kettlebrook and the ground is in Kettlebrook Road, 50 yards from the traffic island by the Railway Viaduct and the Snowdome. The ground is signposted from all major roads.

WREXHAM FC

Founded: 1872
Nickname: 'Red Dragons'
Ground: Racecourse Ground, Mold Road, Wrexham, North Wales LL11 2AH
Ground Capacity: 10,500 (all seats) at present as the ground undergoes re-development
Record Attendance: 34,445 (26th January 1957)

Pitch Size: 111 × 71 yards
Colours: Red shirts with White shorts
Telephone Nº: (01978) 262129
Fax Number: (01978) 357821
Web Site: www.wrexhamafc.co.uk

GENERAL INFORMATION

Car Parking: Town car parks are nearby and also Glyndwr University (Mold End)
Coach Parking: By Police direction
Nearest Railway Station: Wrexham General (adjacent)
Nearest Bus Station: Wrexham (King Street)
Club Shop: At the corner of Mold Road and Crispin Lane
Opening Times: Monday to Saturday 9.00am to 5.00pm
Telephone Nº: (01978) 262129
Police Telephone Nº: (01978) 290222

GROUND INFORMATION

Away Supporters' Entrances & Sections:
Turnstiles 1-4 for the Yale Stand

ADMISSION INFO (2010/2011 PRICES)

Adult Seating: £17.00 – £18.00
Child Seating: £5.00
Senior Citizen Seating: £12.00
Note: Tickets are cheaper when purchased in advance
Programme Price: £3.00

DISABLED INFORMATION

Wheelchairs: 35 spaces in the Mold Road Stand
Helpers: One helper admitted per wheelchair
Prices: £10.00 for the disabled. Free of charge for helpers
Disabled Toilets: Available in the disabled section
Contact: (01978) 262129 (Bookings are preferred)

Travelling Supporters' Information:
Routes: From the North and West: Take the A483 and the Wrexham bypass to the junction with the A541. Branch left at the roundabout and follow Wrexham signs into Mold Road; From the East: Take the A525 or A534 into Wrexham then follow the A541 signs into Mold Road; From the South: Take the the M6, then the M54 and follow the A5 and A483 to the Wrexham bypass and the junction with the A541. Branch right at the roundabout and follow signs for the Town Centre.

YORK CITY FC

Founded: 1922
Nickname: 'Minstermen'
Ground: Bootham Crescent, York   YO30 7AQ
Ground Capacity: 9,496
Seating Capacity: 3,509
Record Attendance: 28,123 (5th March 1938)
Pitch Size: 115 × 74 yards

Colours: Red shirts with Blue shorts
Telephone N°: (01904) 624447
Ticket Office: (01904) 624447 Extension 1
Fax Number: (01904) 631457 or 08712 515800
Web Site: www.ycfc.net

GENERAL INFORMATION

Car Parking: Street parking
Coach Parking: By Police direction
Nearest Railway Station: York (1 mile)
Nearest Bus Station: York
Club Shop: At the ground
Opening Times: Weekdays 10.30am – 2.30pm and
Saturday Matchdays 1.00pm–3.00pm and 4.40pm–5.30pm;
Evening matches open from 6.00pm
Telephone N°: (01904) 624447 Extension 4
Police Telephone N°: 0845 606-0247

GROUND INFORMATION

Away Supporters' Entrances & Sections:
Grosvenor Road turnstiles for Grosvenor Road End

ADMISSION INFO (2010/2011 PRICES)

Adult Standing: £14.00
Adult Seating: £15.00 – £17.00
Child Standing: £9.00
Child Seating: £6.00 – £11.00
Note: Concessions are available in the Family Stand
Programme Price: £3.00

DISABLED INFORMATION

Wheelchairs: 18 spaces in total for Home and Away fans in the disabled section, in front of the Social Club
Helpers: One helper admitted per disabled person
Prices: £14.00 for the disabled. Free of charge for helpers
Disabled Toilets: Available at entrance to the disabled area
Contact: (01904) 624447 (Ext. 1) (Bookings not necessary)

Travelling Supporters' Information:
Routes: From the North: Take the A1 then the A59 following signs for York. Cross the railway bridge and turn left after 2 miles into Water End. Turn right at the end following City Centre signs for nearly ½ mile then turn left into Bootham Crescent; From the South: Take the A64 and turn left after Buckles Inn onto the Outer Ring Road. Turn right onto the A19, follow City Centre signs for 1½ miles then turn left into Bootham Crescent; From the East: Take the Outer Ring Road turning left onto the A19. Then as from the South; From the West: Take the Outer Ring Road turning right onto the A19. Then as from the South.

THE FOOTBALL CONFERENCE BLUE SQUARE NORTH

Address

Third Floor, Wellington House,
31-34 Waterloo Street, Birmingham   B2 5TJ

Phone (0121) 214-1950

Web site   www.footballconference.co.uk

Clubs for the 2010/2011 Season

AFC TELFORD UNITED

Founded: 2004
Former Names: Formed after Telford United FC went out of business. TUFC were previously known as Wellington Town FC
Nickname: 'The Bucks'
Ground: The New Bucks Head Stadium, Watling Street, Wellington, Telford TF1 2TU
Record Attendance: 13,000 (1935)

Pitch Size: 110 × 74 yards
Colours: White shirts with Black shorts
Telehone Nº: (01952) 640064
Fax Number: (01952) 640021
Ground Capacity: 5,780
Seating Capacity: 2,280
Web site: www.telfordutd.co.uk

GENERAL INFORMATION
Supporters Club: None
Car Parking: At the ground
Coach Parking: At the ground
Nearest Railway Station: Wellington
Nearest Bus Station: Wellington
Club Shop: At the ground
Opening Times: Tuesdays and Thursdays 4.00pm to 6.00pm and Saturday Matchdays from 1.30pm
Telephone Nº: –
Police Telephone Nº: 0300 333-3000

GROUND INFORMATION
Away Supporters' Entrances & Sections:
Frank Nagington Stand on the rare occasions when segregation is used

ADMISSION INFO (2010/2011 PRICES)
Adult Standing: £11.00
Adult Seating: £11.00
Child Standing: £1.00
Child Seating: £1.00
Senior Citizen/Concessionary Standing: £8.00
Senior Citizen/Concessionary Seating: £8.00
Programme Price: £2.00

DISABLED INFORMATION
Wheelchairs: Accommodated at the both ends of the ground
Helpers: Admitted
Prices: Normal prices apply
Disabled Toilets: Available
Contact: (01952) 640064   (Bookings are not necessary)

Travelling Supporters' Information:
Routes: Exit the M54 at Junction 6 and take the A518. Go straight on at the first roundabout, take the second exit at the next roundabout then turn left at the following roundabout. Follow the road round to the right then turn left into the car park.

ALFRETON TOWN FC

Founded: 1959
Former Names: None
Nickname: 'Reds'
Ground: The Impact Arena, North Street, Alfreton, Derbyshire DE55 7FZ
Record Attendance: 5,023 vs Matlock Town (1960)
Pitch Size: 110 × 75 yards

Colours: Red shirts and shorts
Telephone Nº: (0115) 939-2090
Fax Number: (0115) 949-1846
Ground Capacity: 5,000
Seating Capacity: 1,600
Web site: www.alfretontownfc.com

GENERAL INFORMATION

Supporters Club: Mark Thorpe, c/o Social Club
Telephone Nº: (01773) 836251
Car Parking: At the ground
Coach Parking: Available close to the ground
Nearest Railway Station: Alfreton (½ mile)
Nearest Bus Station: Alfreton (5 minutes walk)
Club Shop: At the ground
Opening Times: Matchdays only
Telephone Nº: (01773) 830277
Police Telephone Nº: (01773) 570100

GROUND INFORMATION

Away Supporters' Entrances & Sections:
Segregation not usual but please check prior to the game

ADMISSION INFO (2010/2011 PRICES)

Adult Standing: £10.00
Adult Seating: £10.00
Senior Citizen/Junior Standing: £5.00
Senior Citizen/Junior Seating: £5.00
Programme Price: £2.00

DISABLED INFORMATION

Wheelchairs: Accommodated at the front of the Stand
Helpers: Admitted
Prices: Please phone the club for information
Disabled Toilets: Available
Contact: (01773) 830277 (Bookings are not necessary)

Travelling Supporters' Information:
Routes: Exit the M1 at Junction 28 and take the A38 signposted for Derby. After 2 miles take the sliproad onto the B600 then go right at the main road towards the town centre. After ½ mile turn left down North Street and the ground is on the right after 200 yards.

BLYTH SPARTANS FC

Founded: 1899
Former Names: None
Nickname: 'Spartans'
Ground: Croft Park, Blyth, Northumberland, NE24 3JE
Record Attendance: 10,186
Pitch Size: 110 × 70 yards

Colours: Green and White striped shirts, Black shorts
Telephone Nº: (01670) 352373 (Office)
Fax Number: (01670) 545592
Ground Capacity: 6,000
Seating Capacity: 540
Web site: www.blythspartansafc.co.uk

GENERAL INFORMATION
Supporters Club: Bobby Bell, c/o Club
Telephone Nº: (01670) 352373
Car Parking: At the ground
Coach Parking: At the ground
Nearest Railway Station: Newcastle
Nearest Bus Station: Blyth (5 minutes walk)
Club Shop: At the ground
Opening Times: Matchdays only
Telephone Nº: c/o (01670) 336379
Police Telephone Nº: (01661) 872555

GROUND INFORMATION
Away Supporters' Entrances & Sections:
No usual segregation

ADMISSION INFO (2010/2011 PRICES)
Adult Standing: £10.00
Adult Seating: £11.50
Concessionary Standing: £5.50
Concessionary Seating: £6.50
Note: Under-10s are admitted free of charge when accompanied by a paying adult
Programme Price: £2.00

DISABLED INFORMATION
Wheelchairs: Accommodated
Helpers: Please phone the club for information
Prices: Please phone the club for information
Disabled Toilets: Yes
Contact: (01670) 352373 (Bookings are necessary)

Travelling Supporters' Information:
Routes: Pass through the Tyne Tunnel and take the left lane for Morpeth (A19/A1). At the 2nd roundabout (after approximately 7 miles) take full right turn for the A189 (signposted Ashington). After 2 miles take the slip road (A1061 signposted Blyth). Follow signs for Blyth turning left at the caravan site. At the 2nd roundabout turn right and the ground is on the left.

BOSTON UNITED FC

Founded: 1933
Former Names: Boston Town FC & Boston Swifts FC
Nickname: 'The Pilgrims'
Ground: Jakeman's Stadium, York Street, Boston, PE21 6JN
Ground Capacity: 6,613 Seating Capacity: 2,000
Pitch Size: 112 × 72 yards

Record Attendance: 10,086 (1955)
Colours: Amber and Black shirts, Black shorts
Telephone Nº: (01205) 364406 (Office)
Matchday Info: (01205) 364406 or 07860 663299
Fax Number: (01205) 354063
Web Site: www.bufc.co.uk
E-mail: admin@bufc.co.uk

GENERAL INFORMATION

Car Parking: Permit holders only
Coach Parking: Available near to the ground
Nearest Railway Station: Boston (1 mile)
Nearest Bus Station: Boston Coach Station (¼ mile)
Club Shop: In the car park at the ground
Opening Times: Weekdays from 9.00am to 5.00pm and Saturday Matchdays from 11.00am to 5.00pm
Telephone Nº: (01205) 364406
Police Telephone Nº: (01205) 366222

GROUND INFORMATION

Away Supporters' Entrances & Sections:
York Street Entrances 3 & 4

ADMISSION INFO (2010/2011 PRICES)

Adult Standing: £11.00
Adult Seating: £13.00
Child Standing: £4.00
Child Seating: £5.00
Senior Citizen Standing: £8.00
Senior Citizen Seating: £9.00
Programme Price: £2.50

DISABLED INFORMATION

Wheelchairs: 7 spaces available for home fans, 4 spaces for away fans below the Main Stand at the Town End
Helpers: One helper admitted per disabled fan
Prices: £10.00 for the disabled. Free of charge for helpers
Disabled Toilets: Available in the Town End Terrace
Contact: (01205) 364406 (Bookings are necessary)

Travelling Supporters' Information:
From the North: Take the A17 from Sleaford, bear right after the railway crossing to the traffic lights over the bridge. Go forward through the traffic lights into York Street for the ground; From the South: Take the A16 from Spalding and turn right at the traffic lights over the bridge. Go forward through the next traffic lights into York Street for the ground.

CORBY TOWN FC

Founded: 1948
Former Names: None
Nickname: 'The Steelmen'
Ground: Rockingham Triangle Stadium,
Rockingham Road, Corby   NN17 2AE
Record Attendance: 2,240 vs Watford (1986/87)
Pitch Size: 110 × 70 yards

Colours: Black and White Striped shirts, Black shorts
Telephone Nº: (01536) 406640
Fax Number: (0116) 237-6162
Ground Capacity: 3,000
Seating Capacity: 964
Web site: www.corbytown.net

GENERAL INFORMATION
Supporters Club: None
Car Parking: Spaces for 250 cars at the ground
Coach Parking: At the ground
Nearest Railway Station: Kettering (8 miles)
Nearest Bus Station: Corby Town Centre
Club Shop: At the ground
Opening Times: Matchdays only – 1 hour before kick-off
Telephone Nº: (01536) 406640
Police Telephone Nº: (01252) 324545

GROUND INFORMATION
Away Supporters' Entrances & Sections:
No usual segregation

ADMISSION INFO (2010/2011 PRICES)
Adult Standing: £10.00
Adult Seating: £10.00
Child Standing: £2.00
Child Seating: £2.00
Senior Citizen Standing: £6.00
Senior Citizen Seating: £6.00
Programme Price: £2.00

DISABLED INFORMATION
Wheelchairs: Accommodated
Helpers: Admitted
Prices: Normal prices apply for disabled fans. Helpers are
admitted free of charge
Disabled Toilets: Available
Contact: (01536) 406640   (Bookings are not necessary)

Travelling Supporters' Information:
Routes: From the North & East: Exit the A1(M) at junction 17 and take the A605 to Oundle then the A427 to Little Weldon. At the roundabout take the A6116 towards Rockingham and the ground is adjacent to Rockingham Castle near the junction with the A6003; From the South: Take the A14 to the junction with the A6116 and continue to the junction with the A6003 at Rockingham Castle; From the West: Take the A14 or A427 to the A6003 then continue north towards Rockingham to the junction with the A6116 where the ground is on the left.

DROYLSDEN FC

Founded: 1892
Former Names: None
Nickname: 'The Bloods'
Ground: Butchers Arms, Market Street, Droylsden, Manchester M43 7AY
Record Attendance: 5,400 (1973)
Pitch Size: 110 × 70 yards

Colours: Red shirts with Red shorts
Telephone Nº: (0161) 370-1426
Daytime Phone Nº: (0161) 370-1426
Fax Number: (0161) 370-8341
Ground Capacity: 3,500
Seating Capacity: 500
Web site: www.droylsdenfc.com

GENERAL INFORMATION
Supporters Club: c/o Club
Telephone Nº: –
Car Parking: Street parking only
Coach Parking: At the ground
Nearest Railway Station: Manchester Piccadilly
Nearest Bus Station: Ashton
Club Shop: At the ground
Opening Times: Matchdays only
Telephone Nº: (0161) 370-1426
Police Telephone Nº: (0161) 330-8321

GROUND INFORMATION
Away Supporters' Entrances & Sections:
No usual segregation

ADMISSION INFO (2010/2011 PRICES)
Adult Standing: £10.00
Adult Seating: £10.00
Concessionary Standing: £6.00
Concessionary Seating: £6.00
Note: Under-14s are admitted free of charge when accompanied by a paying adult
Programme Price: £2.00

DISABLED INFORMATION
Wheelchairs: Accommodated beside the Stand
Helpers: Yes
Prices: Normal prices apply for the disabled and helpers
Disabled Toilets: Available
Contact: (0161) 370-1426 (Bookings are not necessary)

Travelling Supporters' Information:
Routes: Take the Manchester Outer Ring Road M60 and exit at Junction 23. Join the A635 towards Manchester and after the retail park on the left, take the centre lane, then turn right at the traffic lights onto the A662 signposted for Droylsden. At the next traffic lights, turn right onto Market Street and after 150 yards go straight on at the traffic lights. The entrance to the ground is 75 yards on the left.

EASTWOOD TOWN FC

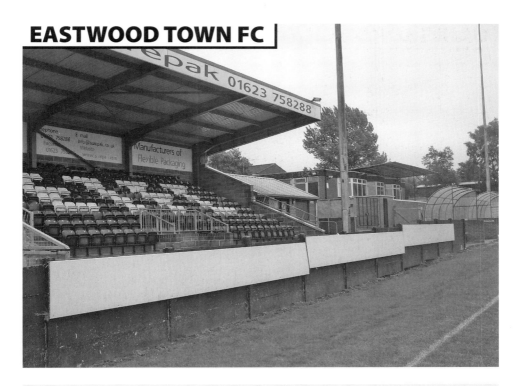

Founded: 1953
Former Names: None
Nickname: 'The Badgers'
Ground: Coronation Park, Chewton Street, Eastwood NG16 3HB
Record Attendance: 2,723 (February 1965)
Pitch Size: 115 × 77 yards

Colours: Shirts are White with Black trim, Black shorts
Clubhouse Telephone Nº: (01773) 715823
Office Telephone Nº: (01773) 711819
Fax Number: (01773) 712301
Ground Capacity: 3,146
Seating Capacity: 645
Web site: www.eastwoodtownfc.co.uk

GENERAL INFORMATION

Car Parking: At the ground
Coach Parking: At the ground
Nearest Railway Station: Langley Mill (1 mile)
Nearest Bus Station: Nottingham
Club Shop: At the ground
Opening Times: Matchdays only
Telephone Nº: (01773) 786186

GROUND INFORMATION

Away Supporters' Entrances & Sections:
No usual segregation

ADMISSION INFO (2010/2011 PRICES)

Adult Standing/Seating: £9.00
Under-16s Standing/Seating: £3.00
Senior Citizen Standing/Seating: £6.00
Note: Under-16s attending with a paying adult are admitted free of charge.
Programme Price: £2.00

DISABLED INFORMATION

Wheelchairs: Accommodated
Helpers: Admitted
Prices: Normal prices apply
Disabled Toilets: Available
Contact: (01773) 715823 (Bookings are not necessary)

Travelling Supporters' Information:
Routes: From the North: Exit the M1 at Junction 27 and take the 3rd exit at the roundabout towards Heanor (A608). Follow the road past the Sandhills Tavern to a T-junction signposted for Brinsley/Heanor and continue along the A608. Follow the road through Brinsley into Eastwood then turn left at the lights into Nottingham Road. Look for the Fire Station on the right, then take the first right into Chewton Street. The Ground is on the right after 150 metres; From the South: Exit the M1 at Junction 26 and follow the A610 towards Ripley. Exit the A610 at the first junction signposted for Ilkeston and turn right onto the B6010, following the signs for Eastwood. Take the first left after the Man In Space pub into Chewton Street. The ground is on the right.

GAINSBOROUGH TRINITY FC

Founded: 1873
Former Names: None
Nickname: 'The Blues'
Ground: Northolme, Gainsborough, Lincolnshire, DN21 2QW
Record Attendance: 9,760 (1948)
Pitch Size: 111 × 71 yards

Colours: Blue shirts and shorts
Telephone Nº: (01427) 613295
Clubhouse Phone Nº: (01427) 613688
Fax Number: (01427) 613295
Ground Capacity: 4,340
Seating Capacity: 504
Web site: www.gainsboroughtrinity.com

GENERAL INFORMATION

Supporters Club: G. Burton, c/o Club
Telephone Nº: (01427) 613688
Car Parking: Street parking and also in a Local Authority Car Park 150 yards from the ground towards the Town Centre
Coach Parking: Available by prior arrangement
Nearest Railway Station: Lea Road (2 miles)
Nearest Bus Station: Heaton Street (1 mile)
Club Shop: At the ground
Opening Times: Matchdays only
Telephone Nº: (01427) 611612
Police Telephone Nº: (01427) 810910

GROUND INFORMATION

Away Supporters' Entrances & Sections:
No usual segregation

ADMISSION INFO (2010/2011 PRICES)

Adult Standing: £10.00
Adult Seating: £11.00
Concessionary Standing: £6.00
Concessionary Seating: £7.00
Under-12s Standing/Seating: £2.00
Children Ages 12 to 16 Standing/Seating: £4.00
Programme Price: £1.50

DISABLED INFORMATION

Wheelchairs: Accommodated
Helpers: Please phone the club for information
Prices: Normal prices for the disabled. Free for helpers
Disabled Toilets: Available in new block adjacent to the Main Stand
Contact: (01427) 613295   (Bookings are not necessary)

Travelling Supporters' Information:
Routes: From the North, South and West: Exit the A1 at Blyth services taking the 1st left through to Bawtry. In Bawtry, turn right at the traffic lights onto the A631 straight through to Gainsborough (approx. 11 miles). Go over the bridge to the second set of traffic lights and turn left onto the A159 (Scunthorpe Road). Follow the main road past Tesco on the right through the traffic lights. The ground is situated on right approximately a third of a mile north of the Town Centre; From the East: Take the A631 into Gainsborough and turn right onto the A159. Then as above.

GLOUCESTER CITY FC

Gloucester City are groundsharing with Cheltenham Town FC for the 2010/2011 season.

Founded: 1889 (**Re-formed**: 1980)
Forner Names: Gloucester YMCA
Nickname: 'The Tigers'
Ground: Abbey Business Stadium, Whaddon Road, Cheltenham, Gloucestershire   GL52 5NA
Ground Capacity: 7,136
Seating Capacity: 4,054

Record Attendance: 8,326 (1956)
Pitch Size: 110 × 72 yards
Colours: Yellow and Black Striped shirts, Black shorts
Telephone Nº: 07813 931781
Web Site: www.gloucestercityafc.com
E-mail: contact@gloucestercityafc.com

GENERAL INFORMATION

Car Parking: No parking is available at the ground.
A Park & Ride scheme runs from Cheltenham Race Course
Coach Parking: Please phone for details
Nearest Railway Station: Cheltenham Spa (2½ miles)
Nearest Bus Station: Cheltenham Royal Well
Club Shop: None
Opening Times: –
Police Telephone Nº: (01242) 528282

GROUND INFORMATION

Away Supporters' Entrances & Sections:
Carlsberg Stand (entrance from Whaddon Road) or the In2Print Stand

ADMISSION INFO (2010/2011 PRICES)

Adult Standing: £12.00
Adult Seating: £12.00
Child Standing: £6.00
Child Seating: £6.00
Concessionary Standing: £6.00
Concessionary Seating: £6.00
Programme Price: £2.00

DISABLED INFORMATION

Wheelchairs: Accommodated in front of the Stagecoach West Stand (use main entrance) and in the In 2 Print Stand
Helpers: Admitted free of charge
Prices: Normal prices apply for disabled fans
Disabled Toilets: Available in the In 2 Print Stand, adjacent to the Stagecoach West Stand and in the Social Club
Contact: 07813 931781

Travelling Supporters' Information:
Routes: The ground is situated to the North-East of Cheltenham, 1 mile from the Town Centre off the B4632 (Prestbury Road) – Whaddon Road is to the East of the B4632 just North of Pittville Circus. Road signs in the vicinity indicate 'Whaddon Road/ Cheltenham Town FC'.

GUISELEY AFC

Founded: 1909
Former Names: None
Nickname: 'The Lions'
Ground: Nethermoor, Otley Road, Guiseley, Leeds, LS20 8BT
Record Attendance: 2,486 (1989/90)
Pitch Size: 110 × 69 yards

Colours: White shirts with Navy Blue shorts
Telephone Nº: (01943) 873223
Social Club Phone Nº: (01943) 872872
Fax Number: (01943) 873223
Ground Capacity: 3,000
Seating Capacity: 500
Web site: www.guiseleyafc.co.uk

GENERAL INFORMATION

Car Parking: At the ground and in Ings Crescent
Coach Parking: At the ground
Nearest Railway Station: Guiseley (5 minute walk)
Nearest Bus Station: Bus Stop outside the ground
Club Shop: At the ground
Opening Times: Matchdays only
Telephone Nº: (01943) 879236 (weekdays)
Postal Sales: Yes
Police Telephone Nº: (01535) 617059

GROUND INFORMATION

Away Supporters' Entrances & Sections:
No usual segregation

ADMISSION INFO (2010/2011 PRICES)

Adult Standing: £9.00
Adult Seating: £9.00
Under-12s Standing: £1.00
Under-12s Seating: £1.00
Concessionary Standing: £5.00
Concessionary Seating: £5.00
Programme Price: £1.50

DISABLED INFORMATION

Wheelchairs: Accommodated by the Players' Entrance
Helpers: Admitted
Prices: Free for both disabled fans and helpers
Disabled Toilets: None
Contact: (01943) 879236 (Bookings are advisable)

Travelling Supporters' Information:
Routes: Exit the M62 at Junction 28 and take the Leeds Ring Road to the roundabout at the junction of the A65 at Horsforth. Turn left onto the A65 and pass through Rawdon to Guiseley keeping Morrison's supermarket on your left. Pass straight through the traffic lights with the Station pub or your right and the ground is on the right after ¼ mile, adjacent to the cricket field.

HARROGATE TOWN FC

Founded: 1919
Former Names: Harrogate FC and Harrogate Hotspurs FC
Nickname: 'Town'
Ground: CNG Stadium, Wetherby Road, Harrogate, HG2 7SA
Record Attendance: 4,280 (1950)

Pitch Size: 107 × 72 yards
Colours: Yellow and Black striped shirts, Black shorts
Telephone Nº: (01423) 880675 or 883671
Club Fax Number: (01423) 880675
Ground Capacity: 3,290
Seating Capacity: 502
Web site: www.harrogatetown.com

GENERAL INFORMATION

Car Parking: Hospital Car Park adjacent
Coach Parking: At the ground
Nearest Railway Station: Harrogate (¾ mile)
Nearest Bus Station: Harrogate
Club Shop: At the ground
Opening Times: Monday to Friday 9.00am to 3.00pm and also on Matchdays
Telephone Nº: (01423) 885525
Police Telephone Nº: (01423) 505541

GROUND INFORMATION

Away Supporters' Entrances & Sections:
No usual segregation

ADMISSION INFO (2010/2011 PRICES)

Adult Standing: £12.00
Adult Seating: £12.00
Concessionary Standing: £8.00
Concessionary Seating: £8.00
Under-15s Standing: £2.00 (when with a paying adult)
Under-15s Seating: £2.00 (when with a paying adult)
Programme Price: £2.00

DISABLED INFORMATION

Wheelchairs: Accommodated at the front of the Main Stand
Helpers: One helper admitted for each disabled fan
Prices: Free of charge for each disabled fan and helper
Disabled Toilets: Available
Contact: (01423) 880675 (Bookings are necessary)

Travelling Supporters' Information:
Routes: From the South: Take the A61 from Leeds and turn right at the roundabout onto the ring road (signposted York). After about 1¼ miles turn left at the next roundabout onto A661 Wetherby Road. The ground is situated ¾ mile on the right; From the West: Take the A59 straight into Wetherby Road from Empress Roundabout and the ground is on the left; From the East & North: Exit the A1(M) at Junction 47, take the A59 to Harrogate then follow the Southern bypass to Wetherby Road for the A661 Roundabout. Turn right towards Harrogate Town Centre and the ground is on the right after ¾ mile.

HINCKLEY UNITED FC

Founded: 1889
Former Names: Formed when Hinckley Athletic FC merged with Hinckley Town FC in 1997 (previously Westfield Rovers FC)
Nickname: 'The Knitters'
Ground: Greene King Stadium, Leicester Road, Hinckley   LE10 3DR
Record Attendance: 3,231 (1st July 2008)

Pitch Size: 110 × 72 yards
Colours: Shirts are Red with Blue trim, Blue shorts
Telephone Nº: (01455) 840088
Contact Number: (01455) 840088
Ground Capacity: 4,329
Seating Capacity: 630
Web site: www.hinckleyunitedfc.co.uk

GENERAL INFORMATION
Supporters Club: c/o Club
Telephone Nº: (01455) 840088
Car Parking: At the ground (£2.00 charge per car)
Coach Parking: At the ground
Nearest Railway Station: Hinckley (2 miles)
Nearest Bus Station: Hinckley
Club Shop: At the ground
Opening Times: Matchdays only
Telephone Nº: (01455) 840088
Police Telephone Nº: (0116) 222-2222

GROUND INFORMATION
Away Supporters' Entrances & Sections:
West Stand and Terrace if required (no usual segregation)

ADMISSION INFO (2010/2011 PRICES)
Adult Standing: £10.00
Adult Seating: £11.00
Under-16s Standing: Free of charge
Under-16s Seating: £1.00
Senior Citizen Standing: £7.00
Senior Citizen Seating: £8.00
Programme Price: £2.00

DISABLED INFORMATION
Wheelchairs: Accommodated
Helpers: Admitted
Prices: Normal prices apply
Disabled Toilets: Yes
Contact: (01455) 840088   (Bookings are not necessary)

Travelling Supporters' Information:
Routes: From the North-West: Take the A5 southbound and take the 1st exit at Dodwells roundabout onto the A47 towards Earl Shilton. Go straight on over 3 roundabouts then take the 3rd exit at the next roundabout onto the B4668. The entrance to the ground is on the right after 200 yards; From the South: Take the A5 northbound and upon reaching Dodwells roundabout take the 2nd exit onto the A47 towards East Shilton. Then as above; From the North-East: Take the M69, exit at Junction 2 and follow the B4669 towards Hinckley. After 2 miles (passing through 2 sets of traffic lights) bear right into Spa Lane then turn right at the next set of traffic lights onto the B4668 towards Earl Shilton. The Stadium is on the left after 1¾ miles.

HYDE FC

Founded: 1919
Former Names: Hyde FC (1885-1917) and Hyde United FC (1917-2010)
Nickname: 'Tigers'
Ground: Tameside Stadium, Ewen Fields, Walker Lane, Hyde, Cheshire   SK14 2SB
Record Attendance: 9,500 (1952)
Pitch Size: 114 × 70 yards

Colours: White shirts with Navy Blue shorts
Telephone Nº: 0871 200-2116 (Matchdays) or 07778 792502 (Secretary)
Fax Number: 0871 200-2118 (Ground); (01270) 212473 (Secretary)
Ground Capacity: 4,250
Seating Capacity: 550
Web site: www.hydefc.co.uk

GENERAL INFORMATION

Supporters Club: Mark Dring, 16 Gainsborough Walk, Denton, Manchester   M34 6NS
Telephone Nº: (0161) 336-8076
Car Parking: 150 spaces available at the ground
Coach Parking: At the ground
Nearest Railway Station: Newton (¼ mile)
Nearest Bus Station: Hyde
Club Shop: At the ground
Opening Times: Matchdays only
Telephone Nº: 0871 200-2116
Police Telephone Nº: (0161) 330-8321

GROUND INFORMATION

Away Supporters' Entrances & Sections:
No usual segregation although it is used as required

ADMISSION INFO (2010/2011 PRICES)

Adult Standing: £10.00
Adult Seating: £12.00
Child Standing: £4.00
Child Seating: £6.00
Senior Citizen Standing: £4.00
Senior Citizen Seating: £6.00
Programme Price: £2.00

DISABLED INFORMATION

Wheelchairs: Accommodated in the disabled area
Helpers: Please phone the club for information
Prices: Please phone the club for information
Disabled Toilets: Yes
Contact: (01270) 212473   (Bookings are not necessary)

Travelling Supporters' Information:
Routes: Exit the M60 at Junction 24 and then exit the M67 at Junction 3 for Hyde. Turn right at the top of the slip road, left at the lights (Morrisons on the left). Turn right at the next set of lights into Lumn Road then turn left at the Give Way sign into Walker Lane. Take the 2nd Car Park entrance near the Leisure Pool and follow the road round for the Stadium.

ILKESTON TOWN FC

Founded: 1945
Former Names: None
Nickname: 'Robins'
Ground: New Manor Ground, Awsworth Road, Ilkeston, Derbyshire   DE7 8JF
Record Attendance: 2,538
Pitch Size: 113 × 74 yards

Colours: Shirts are Red and White halves, Red shorts
Telephone Nº: 07887 832125
Fax Number: (0115) 944-2949
Ground Capacity: 3,029
Seating Capacity: 550
Correspondence: K.Burnand, 2 Woodland Grove, Clowne, Chesterfield   S43 4AT
Web site: www.ilkeston-townfc.co.uk

GENERAL INFORMATION
Supporters Club: A.Middleton, c/o Club
Social Club Nº: (0115) 932-4094
Car Parking: At the ground
Coach Parking: At the ground
Nearest Railway Station: Derby (9 miles)
Nearest Bus Station: Ilkeston
Club Shop: At the ground
Opening Times: Matchdays only
Telephone Nº: (0115) 932-4094
Police Telephone Nº: (0115) 944-0100

GROUND INFORMATION
Away Supporters' Entrances & Sections:
No usual segregation, but can be used if necessary

ADMISSION INFO (2010/2011 PRICES)
Adult Standing: £10.00
Adult Seating: £11.00
Child/Senior Citizen Standing: £5.00
Child/Senior Citizen Seating: £6.00
Programme Price: £2.00

DISABLED INFORMATION
Wheelchairs: Accommodated
Helpers: Please phone the club for information
Prices: Please phone the club for information
Disabled Toilets: Yes
Are Bookings Necessary: No
Contact: (0115) 932-4094

Travelling Supporters' Information:
Routes: Exit the M1 at Junction 26 and take the A610 westwards for 2-3 miles. At the roundabout, turn left to Awsworth then at the next traffic island join the Awsworth Bypass following signs for Ilkeston A6096. After ½ mile turn right into Awsworth Road (signposted Cotmanhay) and the ground is ½ mile on the left.

NUNEATON TOWN FC

Founded: 1937 (Reformed 2008)
Former Names: Nuneaton Borough FC
Nickname: 'Boro'
Ground: Triton Showers Community Arena,
Liberty Way, Attleborough Fields Industrial Estate,
Nuneaton CV11 6RR
Record Attendance: 22,114 (at Manor Park)
Pitch Size: 121 × 77 yards

Colours: Blue shirts and white shorts
Telephone Nº: (024) 7638-5738
Daytime Phone Nº: (024) 7638-5738
Fax Number: (024) 7637-2995
Ground Capacity: 6,000
Seating Capacity: 500
Web site: www.nuneatontownfc.com

GENERAL INFORMATION

Car Parking: On-site car park plus various other parking spaces available on the nearby Industrial Estate
Coach Parking: At the ground
Nearest Railway Station: Nuneaton (2 miles)
Nearest Bus Station: Nuneaton (2 miles)
Club Shop: Yes – The Boro Shop
Opening Times: By appointment and also on matchdays
Telephone Nº: (024) 7638-5738
Police Telephone Nº: (024) 7664-1111

GROUND INFORMATION

Away Supporters' Entrances & Sections: –

ADMISSION INFO (2010/2011 PRICES)

Adult Standing: £10.00
Adult Seating: £12.00
Concessionary Standing: £7.00
Concessionary Seating: £9.00
Programme Price: £2.00

DISABLED INFORMATION

Wheelchairs: Accommodated
Helpers: Please phone the club for information
Prices: Please phone the club for information
Disabled Toilets: Available
Contact: (024) 7638-5738 (Bookings are necessary)

Travelling Supporters' Information:
Routes: From the South, West and North-West: Exit the M6 at Junction 3 and follow the A444 into Nuneaton. At the Coton Arches roundabout turn right into Avenue Road which is the A4254 signposted for Hinckley. Continue along the A4254 following the road into Garrett Street then Eastboro Way then turn left into Townsend Drive. Follow the road round before turning left into Liberty Way for the ground; From the North: Exit the M1 at Junction 21 and follow the M69. Exit the M69 at Junction 1 and take the 4th exit at the roundabout onto the A5 (Tamworth, Nuneaton). At Longshoot Junction, turn left onto the A47, continue to the roundabout and take the 1st exit onto A4254 Eastborough Way. Turn right at the next roundabout into Townsend Drive then immediately right again for Liberty Way.

REDDITCH UNITED FC

Founded: 1891
Former Names: Redditch Town FC
Nickname: 'The Reds'
Ground: Valley Stadium, Bromsgrove Road, Redditch   B97 4RN
Record Attendance: 5,500 (vs Bromsgrove 1954/55)
Pitch Size: 110 × 72 yards

Colours: Red shirts, shorts and socks
Telephone Nº: (01527) 67450
Contact Nº: (01527) 67450
Fax Number: (01527) 67450
Ground Capacity: 5,000
Seating Capacity: 400
Web site: www.redditchutdfc.co.uk

GENERAL INFORMATION
Supporters Club: c/o Club
Telephone Nº: (01527) 67450
Car Parking: At the ground
Coach Parking: At the ground
Nearest Railway Station: Redditch (¼ mile)
Nearest Bus Station: Redditch (¼ mile)
Club Shop: At the ground
Opening Times: Matchdays only

GROUND INFORMATION
Away Supporters' Entrances & Sections:
No segregation

ADMISSION INFO (2010/2011 PRICES)
Adult Standing: £9.00
Adult Seating: £10.00
Senior Citizen Standing: £5.00
Senior Citizen Seating: £6.00
Under-16s Standing/Seating: £1.00
Programme Price: £2.00

DISABLED INFORMATION
Wheelchairs: Accommodated
Helpers: Admitted
Prices: Normal prices apply to both helpers and disabled
Disabled Toilets: Available
Contact: (01527) 67450   (Bookings are not necessary)

Travelling Supporters' Information:
Routes: Exit the M42 at Junction 2 and follow the A441 towards Redditch. Take the 4th exit at the roundabout (signposted Batchley) and turn left at the traffic lights into Birmingham Road. Take the next right into Clive Road then left into Hewell Road. Continue to the T-junction and turn right, passing the Railway Station on the right. Continue through the traffic lights and the ground is situated on the right hand side after about ¼ mile.

SOLIHULL MOORS FC

Founded: 2007
Former Names: Formed by the merger of Solihull Borough FC and Moor Green FC in 2007
Nickname: 'The Moors'
Ground: Damson Park, Damson Parkway, Solihull, B91 2PP
Record Attendance: 2,000 (vs Birmingham City)

Pitch Size: 110 × 75 yards
Colours: White shirts with Black shorts
Telephone N°: (0121) 705-6770
Fax Number: (0121) 711-4045
Ground Capacity: 3,050
Seating Capacity: 280
Web site: www.solihullmoorsfc.co.uk

GENERAL INFORMATION

Supporters Club: Yes
Car Parking: At the ground
Coach Parking: At the ground
Nearest Railway Station: Birmingham International (2 miles)
Nearest Bus Station: Birmingham (5 miles)
Club Shop: At the ground
Opening Times: Matchdays only
Telephone N°: (0121) 705-6770
Police Telephone N°: (0121) 706-8111

GROUND INFORMATION

Away Supporters' Entrances & Sections:
No usual segregation

ADMISSION INFO (2010/2011 PRICES)

Adult Standing: £10.00
Adult Seating: £10.00
Senior Citizen/Junior Standing: £5.00
Senior Citizen/Junior Seating: £5.00
Note: Under-16s can purchase a season ticket for £30.00
Programme Price: £2.00

DISABLED INFORMATION

Wheelchairs: Spaces for 3 wheelchairs are available
Helpers: Admitted
Prices: Normal prices apply
Disabled Toilets: Available
Contact: (0121) 705-6770

Travelling Supporters' Information:
Routes: Exit the M42 at Junction 6 and take the A45 for 2 miles towards Birmingham. Turn left at the traffic lights near the Posthouse Hotel into Damson Parkway (signposted for Landrover/Damsonwood). Continue to the roundabout and come back along the other carriageway to the ground which is situated on the left after about 150 yards.

STAFFORD RANGERS FC |

Founded: 1876
Former Names: None
Nickname: 'The Boro'
Ground: Marston Road, Stafford   ST16 3BX
Record Attendance: 8,523   (4th January 1975)
Pitch Size: 112 × 75 yards

Colours: Black and White striped shirts, Black shorts
Telephone Nº: (01785) 602430
Social Club Nº: (01785) 602432
Ground Capacity: 3,030
Seating Capacity: 527
Web site: www.staffordrangers.co.uk

GENERAL INFORMATION
Supporters Club: c/o Social Club
Telephone Nº: (01785) 602432
Car Parking: At the ground
Coach Parking: Astonfields Road
Nearest Railway Station: Stafford   (1½ miles)
Nearest Bus Station: Stafford
Club Shop: At the ground
Opening Times: Matchdays only
Telephone Nº: (01785) 602430
Police Telephone Nº: (01785) 258151

GROUND INFORMATION
Away Supporters' Entrances & Sections:
Lotus End

ADMISSION INFO (2010/2011 PRICES)
Adult Standing: £11.00
Adult Seating: £13.00
Concessionary Standing: £7.00
Concessionary Seating: £9.00
Children under the age of 12 are admitted free of charge
when accompanying a paying adult
Programme Price: £2.00

DISABLED INFORMATION
Wheelchairs: Accommodated at Marston Road End
Helpers: Admitted
Prices: Concessionary prices for the disabled. Normal prices
for helpers
Disabled Toilets: Available
Contact: (01785) 602430   (Bookings are not necessary)

Travelling Supporters' Information:
Routes: Exit the M6 at Junction 14 and take the slip road signposted 'Stone/Stafford'. Continue to traffic island and go straight
across then take the 3rd exit on the right into Common Road, signposted 'Common Road/Aston Fields Industrial Estate'. Follow
the road to the bridge and bear left over the bridge. The ground is on the right.

STALYBRIDGE CELTIC FC

Founded: 1909
Former Names: None
Nickname: 'Celtic'
Ground: Bower Fold, Mottram Road, Stalybridge, Cheshire   SK15 2RT
Record Attendance: 9,753 (1922/23)
Pitch Size: 109 × 70 yards

Colours: Blue shirts, White shorts and Blue socks
Telephone Nº: (0161) 338-2828
Daytime Phone Nº: (0161) 338-2828
Fax Number: (0161) 338-8256
Ground Capacity: 6,108
Seating Capacity: 1,155
Web site: www.stalybridgeceltic.co.uk

GENERAL INFORMATION

Supporters Club: Bob Rhodes, c/o Club
Telephone Nº: (01457) 764044
Car Parking: At the ground
Coach Parking: At the ground
Nearest Railway Station: Stalybridge (1 mile)
Nearest Bus Station: Stalybridge town centre
Club Shop: At the ground
Opening Times: Matchdays only
Telephone Nº: (0161) 338-2828
Police Telephone Nº: (0161) 872-5050

GROUND INFORMATION

Away Supporters' Entrances & Sections:
Lockwood & Greenwood Stand on the few occasions when segregation is required. No usual segregation

ADMISSION INFO (2010/2011 PRICES)

Adult Standing: £10.00
Adult Seating: £10.00
Under-14s Standing/Seating: Free of charge
Concessionary Standing: £6.00
Concessionary Seating: £6.00
Programme Price: £2.00

DISABLED INFORMATION

Wheelchairs: 20 spaces available each for home and away fans at the side of the Stepan Stand. A further 9 spaces available in the new Lord Tom Pendry Stand
Helpers: Please phone the club for information
Prices: Please phone the club for information
Disabled Toilets: Available at the rear of the Stepan Stand and at the side of the Lord Tom Pendry Stand
Contact: (0161) 338-2828   (Bookings are necessary)

Travelling Supporters' Information:
Routes: From the Midlands and South: Take the M6, M56, M60 and M67, leaving at the end of the motorway. Go across the roundabout to the traffic lights and turn left. The ground is approximately 2 miles on the left before the Hare & Hounds pub; From the North: Exit the M62 at Junction 18 onto the M60 singposted for Ashton-under-Lyne. Follow the M60 to Junction 24 and join the M67, then as from the Midlands and South.

VAUXHALL MOTORS FC

Founded: 1963
Former Names: Vauxhall GM FC
Nickname: 'Motormen'
Ground: Rivacre Park, Rivacre Road, Hooton, Ellesmere Port, Cheshire CH66 1NJ
Record Attendance: 1,500 (1987)
Pitch Size: 117 × 78 yards
Colours: White shirts with Blue shorts

Telephone Nº: (0151) 328-1114 (Ground)
Ground Capacity: 3,306
Seating Capacity: 266
Contact: Carole Paisey, 31 South Road, West Kirby, Wirral CH48 3HG
Contact Phone and Fax Nº: (0151) 625-6936
Web site: www.vmfc.com
E-mail: office@vmfc.com

GENERAL INFORMATION
Supporters Club: At the ground
Telephone/Fax Nº: (0151) 328-1114
Car Parking: At the ground
Coach Parking: At the ground
Nearest Railway Station: Overpool
Nearest Bus Station: Ellesmere Port
Club Shop: At the ground
Opening Times: Matchdays only
Telephone Nº: –

GROUND INFORMATION
Away Supporters' Entrances & Sections:
No usual segregation

ADMISSION INFO (2010/2011 PRICES)
Adult Standing/Seating: £8.00
Child Seating: £3.00
Child Standing: Free of charge
Senior Citizen Standing/Seating: £5.00
Programme Price: £2.00

DISABLED INFORMATION
Wheelchairs: Accommodated as necessary
Helpers: Admitted
Prices: Normal prices for the disabled. Free for carers
Disabled Toilets: Available
Contact: – (Bookings are not necessary)

Travelling Supporters' Information:
Routes: Exit the M53 at Junction 5 and take the A41 towards Chester. Turn left at the first set of traffic lights into Hooton Green. Turn left at the first T-junction then right at the next T-junction into Rivacre Road. The ground is situated 250 yards on the right.

WORCESTER CITY FC

Founded: 1902
Former Names: Berwick Rangers FC
Nickname: 'The City'
Ground: St. Georges Lane, Worcester   WR1 1QT
Record Attendance: 17,042 (1958/59)
Pitch Size: 110 × 75 yards

Colours: Blue and White shirts, Royal Blue shorts
Telephone Nº: (01905) 23003
Fax Number: (01905) 26668
Ground Capacity: 4,500
Seating Capacity: 1,100
Web site: www.worcestercityfc.co.uk

GENERAL INFORMATION

Supporters Club: P. Gardner, c/o Club
Telephone Nº: –
Car Parking: Street parking
Coach Parking: Street parking
Nearest Railway Station: Foregate Street (1 mile)
Nearest Bus Station: Crowngate Bus Station
Club Shop: At the ground
Opening Times: Monday to Friday and Matchdays from 10.00am to 5.00pm
Telephone Nº: (01905) 23003
Police Telephone Nº: (01905) 723888

GROUND INFORMATION

Away Supporters' Entrances & Sections:
Turnstile at the Canal End when segregation is in force for Canal End accommodation

ADMISSION INFO (2010/2011 PRICES)

Adult Standing: £11.00
Adult Seating: £12.00
Under-16s Standing: £3.00
Under-16s Seating: £3.00
Senior Citizen Standing: £7.00
Senior Citizen Seating: £8.00
Programme Price: £2.50

DISABLED INFORMATION

Wheelchairs: 3 covered spaces available
Helpers: Please phone the club for information
Prices: Please phone the club for information
Disabled Toilets: None
Contact: (01905) 23003   (Bookings are necessary)

Travelling Supporters' Information:
Routes: Exit the M5 at Junction 6 and take the A449 Kidderminster Road. Follow to the end of the dual carriageway and take the second exit at the roundabout for Worcester City Centre. At the first set of traffic lights turn right into the town centre. The 3rd turning on the left is St. Georges Lane.

WORKINGTON AFC

Founded: 1884 (Reformed 1921)
Former Names: None
Nickname: 'Reds'
Ground: Borough Park, Workington   CA14 2DT
Record Attendance: 21,000 (vs Manchester United)
Pitch Size: 110 × 71 yards

Colours: Red shirts and shorts
Telephone Nº: (01900) 602871
Fax Number: (01900) 67432
Ground Capacity: 3,100
Seating Capacity: 500
Web site: www.workingtonafc.com

GENERAL INFORMATION
Supporters Club: Yes
Car Parking: Car Park next to the ground
Coach Parking: At the ground
Nearest Railway Station: Workington (¼ mile)
Nearest Bus Station: Workington (½ mile)
Club Shop: At the ground
Opening Times: Matchdays only
Telephone Nº: (01946) 832710

GROUND INFORMATION
Away Supporters' Entrances & Sections:
No usual segregation

ADMISSION INFO (2010/2011 PRICES)
Adult Standing: £12.00
Adult Seating: £12.00
Senior Citizen/Junior/Student Standing: £7.00
Senior Citizen/Junior/Student Seating: £7.00
Note: Under-5s are admitted free of charge
Programme Price: £2.00

DISABLED INFORMATION
Wheelchairs: Accommodated
Helpers: Admitted
Prices: Normal prices apply
Disabled Toilets: Available
Contact: (01900) 602871   (Bookings are not necessary)

Travelling Supporters' Information:
Routes: Exit the M6 at Junction 40 and take the A66 towards Keswick and Workington. Upon reaching Workington, continue until you reach the traffic lights at a T-junction. Turn left then right through the Town Centre. Bear right when approaching the railway station and proceed straight on. The entrance to the ground is opposite the Tesco store.

THE FOOTBALL CONFERENCE BLUE SQUARE SOUTH

Address

Third Floor, Wellington House,
31-34 Waterloo Street, Birmingham   B2 5TJ

Phone (0121) 214-1950

Web site   www.footballconference.co.uk

Clubs for the 2010/2011 Season

BASINGSTOKE TOWN FC |

Founded: 1896
Former Names: None
Nickname: 'Dragons'
Ground: The Camrose Ground, Western Way, Basingstoke, Hants. RG22 6EZ
Record Attendance: 5,085 (25th November 1997)
Pitch Size: 110 × 70 yards

Colours: Yellow and Blue shirts with Blue shorts
Telephone Nº: (01256) 327575
Fax Number: (01256) 869997
Social Club Nº: (01256) 464353
Ground Capacity: 6,000
Seating Capacity: 650
Web site: www.basingstoketown.net

GENERAL INFORMATION
Supporters Club: c/o Club
Telephone Nº: (01256) 327575
Car Parking: 600 spaces available at the ground
Coach Parking: Ample room available at ground
Nearest Railway Station: Basingstoke
Nearest Bus Station: Basingstoke Town Centre (2 miles)
Club Shop: The Camrose Shop
Opening Times: Matchdays only
Telephone Nº: (01256) 327575
Police Telephone Nº: (01256) 473111

GROUND INFORMATION
Away Supporters' Entrances & Sections:
No usual segregation

ADMISSION INFO (2010/2011 PRICES)
Adult Standing: £10.00
Adult Seating: £11.00
Concessionary Standing: £6.00
Concessionary Seating: £7.00
Under-16s Standing: £3.00
Under-16s Seating: £4.00
Programme Price: £2.00

DISABLED INFORMATION
Wheelchairs: 6 spaces are available under cover
Helpers: Admitted
Prices: Normal prices for the disabled. Free for helpers
Disabled Toilets: Yes
Contact: (01256) 327575 (Bookings are not necessary)

Travelling Supporters' Information:
Routes: Exit the M3 at Junction 6 and take the 1st left at the Black Dam roundabout. At the next roundabout take the 2nd exit, then the 1st exit at the following roundabout and the 5th exit at the next roundabout. This takes you into Western Way and the ground is 50 yards on the right.

BISHOP'S STORTFORD FC

Founded: 1874
Former Names: None
Nickname: 'Blues' 'Bishops'
Ground: Woodside Park, Dunmow Road, Bishop's Stortford CM23 5RG
Record Attendance: 3,555 (2000)
Pitch Size: 110 × 70 yards

Colours: Blue and White shirts with Blue shorts
Telephone Nº: (01279) 306456
Fax Number: (01279) 715621
Ground Capacity: 4,000
Seating Capacity: 500
Web site: www.bsfc.co.uk

GENERAL INFORMATION

Car Parking: 500 spaces available at the ground
Coach Parking: At the ground
Nearest Railway Station: Bishop's Stortford
Nearest Bus Station: Bishop's Stortford
Club Shop: At the ground
Opening Times: Matchdays only 1.30pm to 5.00pm
Telephone Nº: (01279) 306456
Police Telephone Nº: –

GROUND INFORMATION

Away Supporters' Entrances & Sections:
No usual segregation

ADMISSION INFO (2010/2011 PRICES)

Adult Standing/Seating: £10.00
Concessionary Standing/Seating: £6.00
Child Standing/Seating: £4.00
Note: Under-12s are admitted free of charge when accompanied by a paying adult.
Programme Price: £2.50

DISABLED INFORMATION

Wheelchairs: Accommodated in the disabled section
Helpers: Admitted
Prices: Free of charge for the disabled and helpers
Disabled Toilets: Yes
Contact: (01279) 306456 (Bookings are not necessary)

Travelling Supporters' Information:
Routes: Exit the M11 at junction 8 and take the A1250 towards Bishop Stortford. Turn left at the first roundabout and the ground is first right opposite the Golf Club (the entrance is between Industrial Units).

BOREHAM WOOD FC

Founded: 1948
Former Names: Boreham Rovers FC and Royal Retournez FC
Nickname: 'The Wood'
Ground: Meadow Park, Broughinge Road, Boreham Wood, Hertfordshire   WD6 5AL
Record Attendance: 4,030 (2002)
Pitch Size: 112 × 72 yards

Colours: White shirts with Black shorts
Telephone Nº: (0208) 953-5097
Fax Number: (0208) 207-7982
Ground Capacity: 4,620
Seating Capacity: 500
Web site: www.borehamwoodfootballclub.co.uk

GENERAL INFORMATION
Supporters Club: None
Car Parking: At the ground
Coach Parking: At the ground
Nearest Railway Station: Elstree & Boreham Wood (1 mile)
Nearest Bus Station: Barnet
Club Shop: At the ground
Opening Times: 11.00am to 10.00pm Monday to Thursday; 11.00am to 6.00pm at weekends
Telephone Nº: (0208) 953-5097
Police Telephone Nº: (0208) 733-5024

GROUND INFORMATION
Away Supporters' Entrances & Sections:
No usual segregation

ADMISSION INFO (2010/2011 PRICES)
Adult Standing: £10.00
Adult Seating: £10.00
Child Standing: £5.00
Child Seating: £5.00
Programme Price: £2.00

DISABLED INFORMATION
Wheelchairs: Accommodated
Helpers: Admitted free of charge
Prices: Normal prices apply for the disabled
Disabled Toilets: None
Contact: (0208) 953-5097   (Bookings are necessary)

Travelling Supporters' Information:
Routes: Exit the M25 at Junction 23 and take the A1 South. After 2 miles, take the Boreham Wood exit onto the dual carriageway and go over the flyover following signs for Boreham Wood for 1 mile. Turn right at the Studio roundabout into Brook Road, then next right into Broughinge Road for the ground.

BRAINTREE TOWN FC

Founded: 1898
Former Names: Manor Works FC, Crittall Athletic FC, Braintree & Crittall Athletic FC and Braintree FC
Nickname: 'The Iron'
Ground: Cressing Road Stadium, Clockhouse Way, Braintree, Essex   CM7 3RD
Record Attendance: 4,000 (May 1952)
Pitch Size: 111 × 78 yards

Ground Capacity: 4,151
Seating Capacity: 556
Colours: Orange shirts and socks with Blue shorts
Telephone Nº: (01376) 345617
Fax Number: (01376) 330976
Correspondence Address: Tom Woodley, 19A Bailey Bridge Road, Braintree   CM7 5TT
Contact Telephone Nº: (01376) 326234
Web site: www.braintreetownfc.org.uk

GENERAL INFORMATION
Supporters Club: c/o Club
Telephone Nº: (01376) 345617
Car Parking: At the ground
Coach Parking: At the ground
Nearest Railway Station: Braintree (1 mile)
Nearest Bus Station: Braintree
Club Shop: At the ground
Opening Times: Matchdays only
Telephone Nº: (01376) 345617

GROUND INFORMATION
Away Supporters' Entrances & Sections: Gates 1-4

ADMISSION INFO (2010/2011 PRICES)
Adult Standing: £12.00
Adult Seating: £13.00
Child Standing: £7.00
Child Seating: £8.00
Programme Price: £2.00

DISABLED INFORMATION
Wheelchairs: Accommodated
Helpers: Admitted
Prices: Normal prices apply
Disabled Toilets: Available
Contact: (01376) 345617

Travelling Supporters' Information:
Routes: Exit the A120 Braintree Bypass at the McDonald's roundabout following signs for East Braintree Industrial Estate. The floodlights at the ground are visible on the left ½ mile into town. Turn left into Clockhouse Way then left again for the ground.

BROMLEY FC

Founded: 1892
Former Names: None
Nickname: 'Lillywhites'
Ground: The Stadium, Hayes Lane, Bromley, Kent, BR2 9EF
Record Attendance: 12,000 (24th September 1949)
Pitch Size: 112 × 72 yards

Colours: White shirts with Black shorts
Telephone Nº: (020) 8460-5291
Fax Number: –
Ground Capacity: 3,300
Seating Capacity: 1,300
Web site: www.bromleyfc.net

GENERAL INFORMATION
Car Parking: 300 spaces available at the ground
Coach Parking: At the ground
Nearest Railway Station: Bromley South (1 mile)
Nearest Bus Station: High Street, Bromley
Club Shop: At the ground
Opening Times: Matchdays only
Telephone Nº: (020) 8460-5291

GROUND INFORMATION
Away Supporters' Entrances & Sections:
No usual segregation

ADMISSION INFO (2010/2011 PRICES)
Adult Standing: £10.00
Adult Seating: £10.00
Child/Senior Citizen Standing: £5.00
Child/Senior Citizen Seating: £5.00
Note: Under-5s are admitted free of charge
Programme Price: £2.00

DISABLED INFORMATION
Wheelchairs: Accommodated
Helpers: Admitted
Prices: Please phone the club for information
Disabled Toilets: Yes
Contact: (0181) 460-5291 (Bookings are necessary)

Travelling Supporters' Information:
Routes: Exit the M25 at Junction 4 and follow the A21 for Bromley and London for approximately 4 miles before forking left onto the A232 signposted for Croydon/Sutton. At the second set of traffic lights turn right into Baston Road (B265) and follow for approximately 2 miles as it becomes Hayes Street and then Hayes Lane. The ground is on the right just after a mini-roundabout.

CHELMSFORD CITY FC

Founded: 1938
Former Names: Chelmsford FC
Nickname: 'City' or 'Clarets'
Ground: Melbourne Park, Salerno Way, Chelmsford, CM1 2EH
Record Attendance: 16,807 (at previous ground)
Pitch Size: 109 × 70 yards

Colours: Claret and White shirts and shorts
Telephone Nº: (01245) 290959
Fax Number: –
Ground Capacity: 3,000
Seating Capacity: 1,400
Web site: www.chelmsfordcityfc.com

GENERAL INFORMATION

Car Parking: Limited space at ground and street parking
Coach Parking: Two spaces available at the ground subject to advance notice
Nearest Railway Station: Chelmsford (2 miles)
Nearest Bus Station: Chelmsford (2 miles)
Club Shop: At the ground
Opening Times: Matchdays only at present
Telephone Nº: (01245) 290959
Police Telephone Nº: (01245) 491212

GROUND INFORMATION

Away Supporters' Entrances & Sections:
No usual segregation

ADMISSION INFO (2010/2011 PRICES)

Adult Standing: £11.00
Adult Seating: £12.00
Child Standing: £3.50
Child Seating: £4.50
Concessionary Standing: £7.00
Concessionary Seating: £8.00
Programme Price: £2.50

DISABLED INFORMATION

Wheelchairs: Spaces for 11 wheelchairs available
Helpers: Admitted
Prices: Same prices as standing admission
Disabled Toilets: Available
Contact: (01245) 290959 (Bookings are necessary)

Travelling Supporters' Information:
Route: The ground is situated next to the only set of high rise flats in Chelmsford which can therefore be used as a landmark. From the A12 from London: Exit the A12 at Junction 15 signposted for Chelmsford/Harlow/A414 and head towards Chelmsford along the dual-carriageway. At the third roundabout, immediately after passing the 'Superbowl' on the left, take the first exit into Westway, signposted for the Crematorium and Widford Industrial Estate. Continue along Westway which becomes Waterhouse Lane after the second set of traffic lights. At the next set of lights (at the gyratory system) take the first exit into Rainsford Road, signposted for Sawbridgeworth A1060. Continue along Rainsford Road then turn right into Chignal Road at the second set of traffic lights. Turn right again into Melbourne Avenue and Salerno Way is on the left at the end of the football pitches.

DARTFORD FC

Founded: 1888
Former Names: None
Nickname: 'The Darts'
Ground: Princes Park Stadium, Grassbanks,
Darenth Road, Dartford   DA1 1RT
Record Attendance: 4,097 (11th November 2006)
Pitch Size: 110 × 71 yards

Colours: White Shirts with Black Shorts
Telephone N°: (01322) 299990
Fax Number: (01322) 299996
Ground Capacity: 4,097
Seating Capacity: 640
Web Site: www.dartfordfc.co.uk

GENERAL INFORMATION
Car Parking: At the ground
Coach Parking: At the ground
Nearest Railway Station: Dartford (½ mile)
Nearest Bus Station: Dartford (½ mile) & Bluewater (2 miles)
Club Shop: At the ground
Opening Times: Matchdays only – 1.00pm to 6.00pm.
Telephone N°: (01322) 299990

ADMISSION INFO (2010/2011 PRICES)
Adult Standing: £12.00
Adult Seating: £12.00
Senior Citizen/Concessionary Standing: £6.00
Senior Citizen/Concessionary Seating: £6.00
Under-12s Standing/Seating: £2.00
Programme Price: £2.00

DISABLED INFORMATION
Wheelchairs: Accommodated
Helpers: Admitted
Prices: Concessionary prices for the disabled and helpers
Disabled Toilets: Available
Contact: (01322) 299991   (Bookings are not necessary)

Travelling Supporters' Information:
Routes: From M25 Clockwise: Exit the M25 at Junction 1B. At the roundabout, take the 3rd exit onto Princes Road (A225) then the second exit at the next roundabout.* Continue downhill to the traffic lights (with the ground on the left), turn left into Darenth Road then take the 2nd left for the Car Park; From M25 Anti-clockwise: Exit the M25 at Junction 2 and follow the A225 to the roundabout. Take the first exit at this roundabout then the 2nd exit at the next roundabout. Then as from * above.

DORCHESTER TOWN FC

Founded: 1880
Former Names: None
Nickname: 'The Magpies'
Ground: The Jewson Stadium, Weymouth Avenue, Dorchester, Dorset   DT1 2RY
Record Attendance: 4,159 (1st January 1999)
Pitch Size: 110 × 80 yards

Colours: White shirts with Black shorts and socks
Telephone Nº: (01305) 262451
Fax Number: (01305) 267623
Ground Capacity: 5,009
Seating Capacity: 710
Web Site: www.dorchestertownfc.co.uk

GENERAL INFORMATION

Supporters Club: H.G. Gill, 39 Thatcham Park, Yeovil, Somerset
Telephone Nº: (01935) 422536
Car Parking: 350 spaces available at the ground (£1.00 fee)
Coach Parking: At the ground
Nearest Railway Station: Dorchester South and West (both 1 mile)
Nearest Bus Station: Nearby
Club Shop: At the ground
Opening Times: During 1st team matchdays only
Telephone Nº: (01305) 262451
Police Telephone Nº: (01305) 251212

GROUND INFORMATION

Away Supporters' Entrances & Sections:
Main Stand side when segregated (not usual)

ADMISSION INFO (2010/2011 PRICES)

Adult Standing: £9.00
Adult Seating: £10.00
Senior Citizen/Child Standing: £5.50
Senior Citizen/Child Seating: £6.50
Under-16s: £2.50 when accompanied by a paying adult
Programme Price: £2.00

DISABLED INFORMATION

Wheelchairs: 10 spaces available each for home and away fans at the North West End of the terracing
Helpers: Admitted
Prices: Normal prices apply
Disabled Toilets: 2 available near the disabled area
Contact: (01305) 262451   (Bookings are not necessary)

Travelling Supporters' Information:
Routes: Take the Dorchester Bypass (A35) from all directions. The ground is on the South side of town, adjacent to a roundabout at the intersection with the A354 to Weymouth. Alternatively, take Weymouth signs from Dorchester Town Centre for 1½ miles.

DOVER ATHLETIC FC

Founded: 1983
Former Names: None
Nickname: 'The Whites'
Ground: Crabble Athletic Ground, Lewisham Road, River, Dover   CT17 0JB
Record Attendance: 4,186 (2002)
Pitch Size: 111 × 73 yards

Colours: White shirts with Black shorts
Telephone No: (01304) 822373
Fax Number: (01304) 821383
Ground Capacity: 6,500
Seating Capacity: 1,000
Web site: www.dover-athletic.co.uk

GENERAL INFORMATION

Supporters Trust: Simon Harris, c/o Club
Telephone No: –
Car Parking: Street parking
Coach Parking: Street parking
Nearest Railway Station: Kearsney (1 mile)
Nearest Bus Station: Pencester Road, Dover (1½ miles)
Club Shop: At the ground
Opening Times: Saturdays 9.00am to 12.00pm
Telephone No: (01304) 822373
Police Telephone No: (01304) 240055

GROUND INFORMATION

Away Supporters' Entrances & Sections:
Segregation only used when required

ADMISSION INFO (2010/2011 PRICES)

Adult Standing: £10.00
Adult Seating: £11.50
Senior Citizen Standing: £7.00
Child Standing/Seating: £5.00   (Under-11s £2.00)
Senior Citizen Standing/Seating: £8.50
Programme Price: £2.50

DISABLED INFORMATION

Wheelchairs: Approximately 20 spaces are available in front of the Family Stand
Helpers: Please phone the club for information
Prices: Please phone the club for information
Disabled Toilets: None
Contact: –   (Bookings are not necessary)

Travelling Supporters' Information:
Routes: Take the A2 to the Whitfield roundabout and take the 4th exit. Travel down the hill to the mini-roundabout then turn left and follow the road for 1 mile to the traffic lights on the hill. Turn sharp right and pass under the railway bridge – the ground is on the left after 300 yards.

EASTLEIGH FC

Photo courtesy of the Southern Daily Echo

Founded: 1946
Former Names: Swaythling Athletic FC and Swaythling FC
Nickname: 'The Spitfires'
Ground: Silverlake Stadium, Ten Acres, Stoneham Lane, Eastleigh SO50 9HT
Record Attendance: 3,104 (2006)
Pitch Size: 112 × 74 yards

Colours: White shirts with Royal Blue shorts
Telephone Nº: (023) 8061-3361
Fax Number: (023) 8061-2379
Ground Capacity: 3,000
Seating Capacity: 512
Web site: www.eastleigh-fc.co.uk
e-mail: commercial@eastleigh-fc.co.uk

GENERAL INFORMATION

Car Parking: Spaces for 450 cars available (hard standing)
Coach Parking: At the ground
Nearest Railway Station: Southampton Parkway (¾ mile)
Nearest Bus Station: Eastleigh (2 miles)
Club Shop: At the ground
Opening Times: Matchdays and during functions only

GROUND INFORMATION

Away Supporters' Entrances & Sections:
No usual segregation

ADMISSION INFO (2010/2011 PRICES)

Adult Standing/Seating: £10.00
Senior Citizen Standing/Seating: £6.00
Under-16s Standing/Seating: £3.00
Under-12s: Free of charge
Programme Price: £2.00

DISABLED INFORMATION

Wheelchairs: Accommodated
Helpers: Admitted
Prices: Normal prices apply
Disabled Toilets: Available
Contact: (023) 8061-3361   (Bookings are not necessary)

Travelling Supporters' Information:
Routes: Exit the M27 at Junction 5 (signposted for Southampton Airport) and take the A335 (Stoneham Way) towards Southampton. After ½ mile, turn right at the traffic lights into Bassett Green Road. Turn right at the next set of traffic lights into Stoneham Lane and the ground is on the right after ¾ mile.

EBBSFLEET UNITED FC

Founded: 1946
Former Names: Gravesend & Northfleet United FC, Gravesend United FC and Northfleet United FC
Nickname: 'The Fleet'
Ground: Stonebridge Road, Northfleet, Gravesend, Kent   DA11 9GN
Record Attendance: 12,063 (1963)

Colours: Reds shirts with White shorts
Telephone Nº: (01474) 533796
Fax Number: (01474) 324754
Pitch Size: 112 × 72 yards
Ground Capacity: 5,258
Seating Capacity: 1,220
Web site: www.ebbsfleetunited.co.uk

GENERAL INFORMATION
Supporters Club: c/o Club
Telephone Nº: (01474) 533796
Car Parking: Ebbsfleet International Car Park C (when available) and also street parking
Coach Parking: At the ground
Nearest Railway Station: Northfleet (5 minutes walk)
Nearest Bus Station: Bus Stop outside the ground
Club Shop: At the ground
Opening Times: Matchdays only
Telephone Nº: (01474) 533796
Police Telephone Nº: (01474) 564346

GROUND INFORMATION
Away Supporters' Entrances & Sections:
Only some games are segregated – contact club for details

ADMISSION INFO (2010/2011 PRICES)
Adult Standing: £11.00
Adult Seating: £13.00
Senior Citizen/Child Standing: £5.00
Senior Citizen/Child Seating: £7.00
Programme Price: £2.50

DISABLED INFORMATION
Wheelchairs: 6 spaces are available in the Disabled Area in front of the Main Stand
Helpers: Admitted free of charge
Prices: Please phone the club for information
Disabled Toilets: Available in the Main Stand
Contact: (01474) 533796   (Bookings are necessary)

Travelling Supporters' Information:
Routes: Take the A2 to the Northfleet/Southfleet exit and follow signs for Northfleet (B262).Go straight on at the first roundabout then take the 2nd exit at the 2nd roundabout into Thames Way and follow the football signs for the ground.

FARNBOROUGH FC |

Founded: 1967   (Re-formed in 2007)
Former Names: Farnborough Town FC
Nickname: 'The Boro'
Ground: The Rushmoor Stadium, Cherrywood Road, Farnborough   GU14 8UD
Record Attendance: 3,581 (1995 – as FTFC)
Pitch Size: 115 × 77 yards

Colours: Yellow and Blue shirts and shorts
Telephone Nº: 0844 807-9900
Fax Number: (01252) 372640
Ground Capacity: 5,600 at present
Seating Capacity: 3,135 (when redevelopment has been completed)
Web site: www.farnboroughfc.co.uk
E-mail contact: steve.duly@farnboroughfc.co.uk

GENERAL INFORMATION

Car Parking: 260 spaces available at the ground with a further 200 spaces at the nearby Sixth Form college
Coach Parking: At the ground
Nearest Railway Stations: Farnborough (Main), Farnborough North, Frimley and Blackwater
Nearest Bus Station: Buses from Farnborough Main stop just outside the ground – please check the web site for details.
Club Shop: At the ground + web sales in the near future
Opening Times: Matchdays only
Telephone Nº: 0844 807-8800
Police Telephone Nº: 08450 454545

GROUND INFORMATION

Away Supporters' Entrances & Sections:
Moor Road entrances and accommodation

ADMISSION INFO (2010/2011 PRICES)

Adult Standing: £10.00
Adult Seating: £10.00
Concessionary Standing: £7.00
Concessionary Seating: £7.00
Under-16s Seating/Standing: Free of charge
Note: In keeping with F.A. Regulations, the Club reserves the right to charge higher prices for F.A. Trophy and F.A. Cup games.
Programme Price: £2.50

DISABLED INFORMATION

Wheelchairs: Spaces available in front of the Main Stand
Helpers: Admitted free of charge
Prices: Concessionary prices charged for disabled fans
Disabled Toilets: To become available shortly after the start of the 2010/11 season
Contact: 0844 807-9900   (Bookings are not necessary)

Travelling Supporters' Information:
Routes: Exit the M3 at Junction 4 and take the A331 signposted for Farnham. After a few hundred yards exit at the second slip road – signposted A325 Farnborough – turn right at the roundabout and cross over the dual carriageway and a small roundabout. Pass the Farnborough Gate shopping centre on your left and at the next roundabout turn left onto the A325. Go over a pelican crossing and at the next set of lights take the right filter lane into Prospect Avenue. At the end of this road turn right at the roundabout into Cherrywood Road. The ground is on the right after ½ mile.

HAMPTON & RICHMOND BOROUGH FC

Founded: 1921
Former Names: Hampton FC
Nickname: 'Beavers'
Ground: Beveree Stadium, Beaver Close,
off Station Road, Hampton, Middlesex TW12 2BT
Record Attendance: 3,500 vs West Ham United
Pitch Size: 113 × 71 yards

Colours: Red shirts with Blue flash, Red shorts
Matchday Phone Nº: (020) 8979-2456
Fax Number: (020) 8979-2456
Ground Capacity: 3,500
Seating Capacity: 300
Web site: www.hamptonfc.net

GENERAL INFORMATION

Supporters Club: Yes
Telephone Nº: (020) 8979-2456
Car Parking: At the ground and street parking
Coach Parking: Contact the Club for information
Nearest Railway Station: Hampton
Nearest Bus Station: Hounslow/Kingston/Fulwell
Club Shop: At the ground
Opening Times: Matchdays only
Telephone Nº: –
Police Telephone Nº: (020) 8577-1212

GROUND INFORMATION

Away Supporters' Entrances & Sections:
No usual segregation

ADMISSION INFO (2010/2011 PRICES)

Adult Standing: £10.00
Adult Seating: £10.00
Senior Citizen/Concessionary Standing: £5.00
Senior Citizen/Concessionary Seating: £5.00
Junior Standing: £3.00 (Ages 4-11)
Junior Seating: £3.00 (Ages 4-11)
Programme Price: £2.50

DISABLED INFORMATION

Wheelchairs: Accommodated
Helpers: Admitted
Prices: Normal prices apply
Disabled Toilets: Available
Contact: (020) 8979-2456 (Bookings are not necessary)

Travelling Supporters' Information:
Routes: From the South: Exit the M3 at Junction 1 and follow the A308 (signposted Kingston). Turn 1st left after Kempton Park into Percy Road. Turn right at the level crossing into Station Road then left into Beaver Close for the ground; From the North: Take the A305 from Twickenham then turn left onto the A311. Pass through Hampton Hill onto Hampton High Street. Turn right at the White Hart pub (just before the junction with the A308), then right into Station Road and right again into Beaver Close.

HAVANT & WATERLOOVILLE FC

Founded: 1998
Former Names: Formed by the amalgamation of Waterlooville FC and Havant Town FC
Nickname: 'The Hawks'
Ground: Westleigh Park, Martin Road, Havant, PO9 5TH
Record Attendance: 5,757 (2006/07)
Pitch Size: 112 × 76 yards

Colours: White shirts and shorts
Telephone Nº: (023) 9278-7822 (Ground)
Fax Number: (023) 9226-2367
Ground Capacity: 5,250
Seating Capacity: 562
Web site: www.havantandwaterlooville.net

GENERAL INFORMATION

Supporters Club: None, but large Social Club
Telephone Nº: (023) 9278-7855
Car Parking: Space for 750 cars at the ground
Coach Parking: At the ground
Nearest Railway Station: Havant (1 mile)
Nearest Bus Station: Town Centre (1½ miles)
Club Shop: At the ground
Opening Times: Daily
Telephone Nº: (023) 9278-7822
Police Telephone Nº: (0845) 454545

GROUND INFORMATION

Away Supporters' Entrances & Sections:
Martin Road End

ADMISSION INFO (2010/2011 PRICES)

Adult Standing: £10.00
Adult Seating: £10.00
Senior Citizen Standing/Seating: £6.00
Note: When accompanied by a paying adult, children under the age of 11 are admitted free of charge
Programme Price: £2.00

DISABLED INFORMATION

Wheelchairs: 12 spaces available in the Main Stand
Helpers: Admitted
Prices: Normal prices for disabled fans. Free for helpers
Disabled Toilets: Two available
Contact: (023) 9226-7276 (Bookings are necessary)

Travelling Supporters' Information:
Routes: From London or the North take the A27 from Chichester and exit at the B2149 turn-off for Havant. Take the 2nd exit off the dual carriageway into Bartons Road and then the 1st right into Martin Road for the ground; From the West: Take the M27 then the A27 to the Petersfield exit. Then as above.

LEWES FC

Founded: 1885
Former Names: None
Nickname: 'Rooks'
Ground: The Dripping Pan, Mountfield Road, Lewes BN7 2XD
Record Attendance: 2,500 (vs Newhaven 26/12/47)
Pitch Size: 109 × 74 yards

Colours: Red & Black striped shirts with Black shorts
Telephone Nº: (01273) 472100
Fax Number: (01273) 483210
Ground Capacity: 3,000
Seating Capacity: 500
Web site: www.lewesfc.com

GENERAL INFORMATION
Supporters Club: c/o Club
Telephone Nº: (01273) 472100
Car Parking: At the ground
Coach Parking: At Lewes Railway Station (adjacent)
Nearest Railway Station: Lewes (adjacent)
Nearest Bus Station: Lewes (½ mile)
Club Shop: At the ground.
Opening Times: Matchdays only

GROUND INFORMATION
Away Supporters' Entrances & Sections:
No usual segregation – otherwise as directed by stewards

ADMISSION INFO (2010/2011 PRICES)
Adult Standing: £10.00
Adult Seating: £10.00
Junior (Under-14s) Standing: £2.00
Junior (Under-14s) Seating: £2.00
Senior Citizen/Under-16s Standing: £5.00
Senior Citizen/Under-16s Seating: £5.00
Programme Price: £2.00

DISABLED INFORMATION
Wheelchairs: Accommodated
Helpers: Admitted
Prices: Normal prices apply for the disabled and helpers
Disabled Toilets: Available
Contact: (01273) 472100

Travelling Supporters' Information:
Routes: From the North: Take the A26 or the A275 to Lewes and follow signs for the Railway Station. Pass the station on the left and take the next left. The ground is adjacent; From the South and West: Take the A27 to the A26 for the Town Centre. Then as above.

MAIDENHEAD UNITED FC

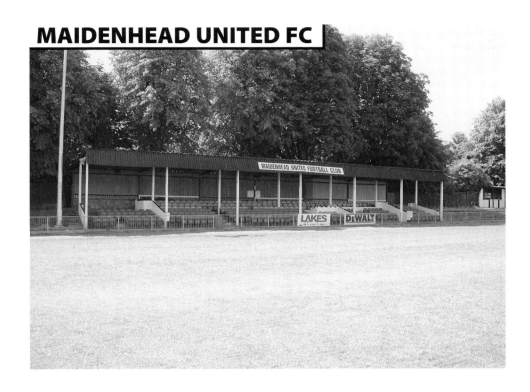

Founded: 1870
Former Names: None
Nickname: 'Magpies'
Ground: York Road, Maidenhead, Berks. SL6 1SF
Record Attendance: 7,920 (1936)
Pitch Size: 110 × 75 yards

Colours: Black and White striped shirts, Black shorts
Telephone Nº: (01628) 636314 (Club)
Contact Number: (01628) 636078
Ground Capacity: 4,500
Seating Capacity: 400
Web site: www.maidenheadunitedfc.co.uk

GENERAL INFORMATION
Supporters Club: c/o Club
Telephone Nº: (01628) 636314
Car Parking: Street parking
Coach Parking: Street parking
Nearest Railway Station: Maidenhead (¼ mile)
Nearest Bus Station: Maidenhead
Club Shop: At the ground
Opening Times: Matchdays only
Telephone Nº: (01628) 624739
Police Telephone Nº: –

GROUND INFORMATION
Away Supporters' Entrances & Sections:
No usual segregation

ADMISSION INFO (2010/2011 PRICES)
Adult Standing: £10.00
Adult Seating: £10.00
Concessionary Standing and Seating: £6.00
Child Standing and Seating: £2.00 (Under-16s)
Programme Price: £1.00

DISABLED INFORMATION
Wheelchairs: Accommodated
Helpers: Admitted
Prices: Normal prices for the disabled. Free for helpers
Disabled Toilets: Available
Contact: (01628) 636078   (Bookings are not necessary)

Travelling Supporters' Information:
Routes: Exit M4 at Junction 7 and take the A4 to Maidenhead. Cross the River Thames bridge and turn left at the 2nd roundabout passing through the traffic lights. York Road is first right and the ground is approximately 300 yards along on the left.

ST. ALBANS CITY FC

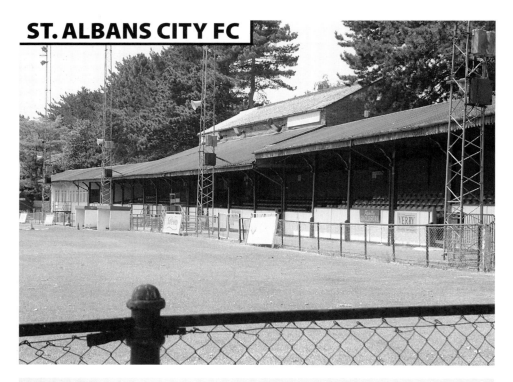

Founded: 1908
Former Names: None
Nickname: 'The Saints'
Ground: Clarence Park, York Road, St. Albans, Hertfordshire AL1 4PL
Record Attendance: 9,757 (27th February 1926)
Pitch Size: 110 × 80 yards

Colours: Blue shirts with Yellow trim, Yellow shorts
Telephone N°: (01727) 864296
Fax Number: (01727) 866235
Ground Capacity: 5,007
Seating Capacity: 667
Web site: www.sacfc.co.uk

GENERAL INFORMATION

Supporters Club: Ian Rogers, c/o Club
Telephone N°: –
Car Parking: Street parking
Coach Parking: In Clarence Park
Nearest Railway Station: St. Albans City (200 yds)
Club Shop: At the ground
Opening Times: Matchdays only
Telephone N°: (01727) 864296
Police Telephone N°: (01727) 276122

GROUND INFORMATION

Away Supporters' Entrances & Sections:
Hatfield Road End when matches are segregated

ADMISSION INFO (2010/2011 PRICES)

Adult Standing: £11.00
Adult Seating: £13.00
Under-14s Standing: £3.00   **OAP/Under-16s:** £6.00
Under-14s Seating: £4.00   **OAP/Under-16s:** £7.00
Note: Under-5s are admitted free of charge
Programme Price: £2.50

DISABLED INFORMATION

Wheelchairs: Accommodated
Helpers: One admitted per disabled supporter
Prices: Free for the disabled, concessionary prices for the helpers
Disabled Toilets: Available inside the building at the York Road End
Contact: (01727) 864296 (Bookings are not necessary)

Travelling Supporters' Information:
Routes: Take the M1 or M10 to the A405 North Orbital Road and at the roundabout at the start of the M10, go north on the A5183 (Watling Street). Turn right along St. Stephen's Hill and carry along into St. Albans. Continue up Holywell Hill, go through two sets of traffic lights and at the end of St. Peter's Street, take a right turn at the roundabout into Hatfield Road. Follow over the mini-roundabouts and at the second set of traffic lights turn left into Clarence Road and the ground is on the left. Park in Clarence Road and enter the ground via the Park or in York Road and use the entrance by the footbridge.

STAINES TOWN FC

Founded: 1892
Former Names: Staines FC, Staines Vale FC, Staines Albany FC, Staines Projectile FC & Staines Lagonda FC
Nickname: 'The Swans'
Ground: Wheatsheaf Park, Wheatsheaf Lane, Staines   TW18 2PD
Record Attendance: 2,860 (2007)
Pitch Size: 110 × 76 yards

Ground Capacity: 3,000
Seating Capacity: 500
Colours: Old Gold and Blue shirts with Blue shorts
Telephone Nº: 0782 506-7232
Correspondence Address: Steve Parsons, 3 Birch Green, Staines   TW18 4HA
Web site: www.stainesmassive.co.uk

GENERAL INFORMATION
Supporters Club: None
Car Parking: Large car park shared with The Thames Club
Coach Parking: At the ground
Nearest Railway Station: Staines (1 mile)
Nearest Bus Station: Staines Central (1 mile)
Club Shop: At the ground
Opening Times: Matchdays only
Telephone Nº: (01784) 225943

GROUND INFORMATION
Away Supporters' Entrances & Sections:
No usual segregation

ADMISSION INFO (2010/2011 PRICES)
Adult Standing: £10.00
Adult Seating: £10.00
Senior Citizen/Junior Standing: £5.00
Senior Citizen/Junior Seating: £5.00
Programme Price: £2.00

DISABLED INFORMATION
Wheelchairs: Accommodated
Helpers: Admitted
Prices: Concessionary prices apply for the disabled
Disabled Toilets: Available
Contact: (01784) 225943

Travelling Supporters' Information:
Routes: Exit the M25 at Junction 13 and take the A30 towards London. At the 'Crooked Billet' roundabout follow signs for Staines Town Centre. Pass under the bridge and bear left, passing the Elmsleigh Centre Car Parks and bear left at the next junction (opposite the Thames Lodge Hotel) into Laleham Road. Pass under the iron railway bridge by the river and continue along for ¾ mile. Turn right by the bollards into Wheatsheaf Lane and the ground is situated on the left by the Thames Club.

THURROCK FC

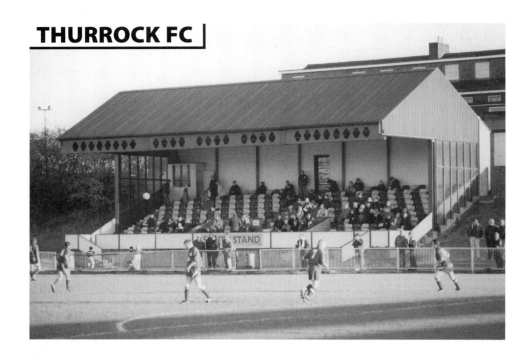

Founded: 1985
Former Names: Purfleet FC
Nickname: 'Fleet'
Ground: Thurrock Hotel, Ship Lane, Grays, Essex, RM19 1YN   **Telephone Nº**: (01708) 865492
Record Attendance: 2,572 (1998)
Pitch Size: 113 × 72 yards

Colours: Yellow and Green shirts with Green shorts
Tel Nº: (01708) 865492 (Clubhouse)
Contact Nº: (01708) 458301 (Secretary)
Fax Number: (01708) 868863
Ground Capacity: 4,200
Seating Capacity: 500
Web site: www.thurrock-fc.com

GENERAL INFORMATION
Car Parking: At the ground
Coach Parking: At the ground
Nearest Railway Station: Purfleet (2 miles)
Nearest Bus Station: Grays Town Centre
Club Shop: At the ground
Opening Times: Matchdays only
Telephone Nº: (01708) 865492
Police Telephone Nº: (01375) 391212

GROUND INFORMATION
Away Supporters' Entrances & Sections:
No usual segregation

ADMISSION INFO (2010/2011 PRICES)
Adult Standing: £12.00
Adult Seating: £12.00
Child Standing: £3.00
Child Seating: £3.00
Senior Citizen Standing: £7.00
Senior Citizen Seating: £7.00
Programme Price: £2.00

DISABLED INFORMATION
Wheelchairs: No special area but accommodated
Helpers: Admitted
Prices: Free for the disabled. Helpers pay normal prices
Disabled Toilets: Available in the Clubhouse
Contact: (01708) 865492 (Bookings are not necessary)

Travelling Supporters' Information:
Routes: Take the M25 or A13 to the Dartford Tunnel roundabout. The ground is then 50 yards on the right along Ship Lane.

WELLING UNITED FC

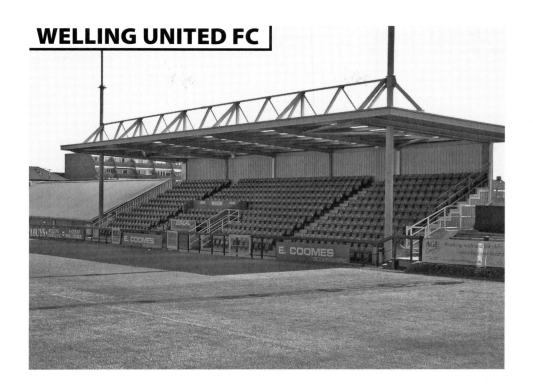

Founded: 1963
Former Names: None
Nickname: 'The Wings'
Ground: Park View Road Ground, Welling, Kent, DA16 1SY
Record Attendance: 4,020 (1989/90)
Pitch Size: 112 × 72 yards

Colours: Shirts are Red with White facings, Red shorts
Telephone Nº: (0208) 301-1196
Daytime Phone Nº: (0208) 301-1196
Fax Number: (0208) 301-5676
Ground Capacity: 4,000
Seating Capacity: 500
Web site: www.wellingunited.com

GENERAL INFORMATION
Supporters Club: –
Car Parking: Street parking only
Coach Parking: Outside of the ground
Nearest Railway Station: Welling (¾ mile)
Nearest Bus Station: Bexleyheath
Club Shop: At the ground
Opening Times: Matchdays only
Telephone Nº: (0208) 301-1196
Police Telephone Nº: (0208) 304-3161

GROUND INFORMATION
Away Supporters' Entrances & Sections:
Accommodation in the Danson Park End

ADMISSION INFO (2010/2011 PRICES)
Adult Standing: £10.00
Adult Seating: £11.00
Senior Citizen/Child Standing: £6.00
Senior Citizen/Child Seating: £7.00
Under-12s: £3.00
Programme Price: £2.00

DISABLED INFORMATION
Wheelchairs: Accommodated at the side of the Main Stand
Helpers: Admitted
Prices: £6.00 for the disabled. Helpers pay normal prices
Disabled Toilets: Yes
Contact: (0208) 301-1196   (Bookings are not necessary)

Travelling Supporters' Information:
Routes: Take the A2 (Rochester Way) from London, then the A221 Northwards (Danson Road) to Bexleyheath. At the end turn left towards Welling along Park View Road and the ground is on the left.

WESTON-SUPER-MARE FC

Founded: 1899
Former Names: Christ Church Old Boys FC
Nickname: 'Seagulls'
Ground: Woodspring Stadium, Winterstoke Road, Weston-super-Mare   BS24 9AA
Record Attendance: 2,623 (vs Woking in F.A. Cup)
Pitch Size: 110 × 70 yards

Colours: White shirts with Black shorts
Telephone Nº: (01934) 621618
Fax Number: (01934) 622704
Ground Capacity: 3,071
Seating Capacity: 320
Web site: www.westonsupermareafc.co.uk

GENERAL INFORMATION

Supporters Club: Joe Varian, 336 Milton Road, Weston-super-Mare
Telephone Nº: (01934) 627929
Car Parking: 140 spaces available at the ground
Coach Parking: At the ground
Nearest Railway Station: Weston-super-Mare (1½ miles)
Nearest Bus Station: Weston-super-Mare (1½ miles)
Club Shop: At the ground
Opening Times: Matchdays only
Telephone Nº: (01934) 621618
Police Telephone Nº: (01275) 818181

GROUND INFORMATION

Away Supporters' Entrances & Sections:
No usual segregation

ADMISSION INFO (2010/2011 PRICES)

Adult Standing/Seating: £10.00
Senior Citizen/Student Standing/Seating: £6.50
Under-16s Standing/Seating: Free of charge (proof of age required) – £2.00 without ID
Programme Price: £2.00

DISABLED INFORMATION

Wheelchairs: Accommodated in a special disabled section
Helpers: Admitted
Prices: Normal prices apply
Disabled Toilets: Two available
Contact: (01934) 621618   (Bookings are not necessary)

Travelling Supporters' Information:
Routes: Exit the M5 at Junction 21 and follow the dual carriageway (A370) to the 4th roundabout (Asda Winterstoke). Turn left, go over the mini-roundabout and continue for 800 yards. The ground is on the right.

WOKING FC

Founded: 1889
Former Names: None
Nickname: 'Cardinals'
Ground: Kingfield Stadium, Kingfield, Woking, Surrey GU22 9AA
Record Attendance: 6,000 (1997)
Pitch Size: 109 × 76 yards

Colours: Shirts are Red & White halves, Black shorts
Telephone Nº: (01483) 772470
Daytime Phone Nº: (01483) 772470
Fax Number: (01483) 888423
Ground Capacity: 6,161
Seating Capacity: 2,511
Web site: www.wokingfc.co.uk

GENERAL INFORMATION

Supporters Club: Mr. G. Burnett (Secretary), c/o Club
Telephone Nº: (01483) 772470
Car Parking: Limited parking at the ground
Coach Parking: At or opposite the ground
Nearest Railway Station: Woking (1 mile)
Nearest Bus Station: Woking
Club Shop: At the ground
Opening Times: Weekdays and Matchdays
Telephone Nº: (01483) 772470
Police Telephone Nº: (01483) 761991

GROUND INFORMATION

Away Supporters' Entrances & Sections:
Kingfield Road entrance for the Tennis Club terrace

ADMISSION INFO (2010/2011 PRICES)

Adult Standing: £12.00
Adult Seating: £12.00
Under-16s/Student Standing: £2.00
Under-16s/Student Seating: £2.00
Senior Citizen Standing: £8.00
Senior Citizen Seating: £8.00
Programme Price: £2.50

DISABLED INFORMATION

Wheelchairs: 8 spaces in the Leslie Gosden Stand and 8 spaces in front of the Family Stand
Helpers: Admitted
Prices: One wheelchair and helper for £8.00
Disabled Toilets: Yes – in the Leslie Gosden Stand and Family Stand area
Contact: (01483) 772470 (Bookings are necessary)

Travelling Supporters' Information:
Routes: Exit the M25 at Junction 10 and follow the A3 towards Guildford. Leave at the next junction onto the B2215 through Ripley and join the A247 to Woking. Alternatively, exit the M25 at Junction 11 and follow the A320 to Woking Town Centre. The ground is on the outskirts of Woking – follow signs on the A320 and A247.

Blue Square Premier
2009/2010 Season

	AFC Wimbledon	Altrincham	Barrow	Cambridge United	Crawley Town	Eastbourne Borough	Ebbsfleet United	Forest Green Rovers	Gateshead	Grays Athletic	Hayes & Yeading United	Histon	Kettering Town	Kidderminster Harriers	Luton Town	Mansfield Town	Oxford United	Rushden & Diamonds	Salisbury City	Stevenage Borough	Tamworth	Wrexham	York City
AFC Wimbledon	■	1-1	0-2	0-0	1-1	2-0	3-0	2-0	2-0	0-2	5-0	4-0	1-2	0-1	1-1	2-0	0-1	0-1	4-0	0-3	0-1	2-2	0-1
Altrincham	0-1	■	0-1	0-2	0-0	3-0	1-1	2-2	3-2	1-1	3-2	2-1	2-0	3-2	0-1	1-2	0-1	2-2	5-0	0-1	0-0	1-3	0-0
Barrow	2-2	0-3	■	0-1	4-1	3-2	2-0	1-1	3-3	2-2	1-1	0-0	0-2	1-0	0-1	3-1	1-1	1-6	0-1	0-0	1-0	2-1	0-0
Cambridge United	2-2	0-0	0-2	■	0-1	0-1	4-0	7-0	3-0	3-0	4-1	2-1	0-2	2-0	3-4	3-2	1-1	2-2	3-1	1-3	2-0	2-0	0-1
Crawley Town	2-1	1-0	0-1	1-0	■	2-2	2-1	3-1	1-4	1-1	1-0	2-0	2-1	2-2	2-1	0-2	1-2	2-1	2-0	0-3	2-0	1-0	3-1
Eastbourne Borough	1-0	2-2	2-1	2-2	0-2	■	1-2	1-0	2-1	2-2	3-1	1-1	0-1	0-0	1-1	1-2	1-0	1-1	0-1	0-6	1-1	2-1	3-1
Ebbsfleet United	2-2	1-2	1-4	1-3	0-0	3-2	■	4-3	2-0	2-1	1-2	0-1	1-2	0-0	1-6	2-1	0-0	1-2	2-1	0-1	0-1	1-0	
Forest Green Rovers	2-5	4-3	1-0	1-1	1-0	1-1	0-0	■	1-0	2-1	0-0	2-0	1-1	0-1	1-0	1-4	0-1	3-1	1-1	3-4	0-2	2-1	
Gateshead	1-0	1-0	2-1	2-0	2-1	3-0	1-3	3-1	■	3-0	0-0	0-3	0-2	0-2	0-1	1-3	0-1	0-0	2-1	0-1	1-1	1-0	1-2
Grays Athletic	2-4	0-3	3-3	2-0	2-3	1-0	0-3	2-1	0-0	■	0-0	0-1	0-0	1-3	0-2	1-1	0-4	0-3	0-2	1-2	1-0	0-2	0-4
Hayes & Yeading United	1-0	1-2	1-1	3-0	2-1	1-1	4-2	2-3	3-2	4-0	■	0-2	1-2	2-2	2-3	1-1	2-1	1-6	3-4	1-1	2-2	0-1	1-1
Histon	1-3	0-0	2-2	1-1	0-1	2-0	5-2	0-0	0-0	3-3		■	1-0	1-1	0-2	5-4	1-0	2-0	0-2	1-0	0-1	0-1	0-1
Kettering Town	1-2	2-0	2-1	0-1	1-1	4-0	0-2	4-0	2-0	0-1	1-1		■	0-2	0-2	2-2	1-1	0-3	1-2	1-1	0-0	2-2	0-1
Kidderminster Harriers	0-1	3-0	1-2	1-0	1-0	0-2	2-2	2-1	3-2	4-1	1-0	3-0	0-1	■	1-2	3-1	3-1	1-1	0-1	0-2	1-1	2-2	0-1
Luton Town	1-2	0-0	1-0	2-2	3-0	4-1	2-3	2-1	2-1	6-0	8-0	6-3	0-1	3-1	■	4-1	2-1	0-2	4-0	0-1	2-1	1-0	2-1
Mansfield Town	0-1	1-1	4-1	2-1	4-0	1-1	3-0	1-0	0-2	3-1	1-1	0-0	3-3	0-0	2-1	■	3-2	4-2	2-3	0-1	1-1	0-1	2-1
Oxford United	2-0	1-0	1-0	0-0	3-1	4-0	4-2	0-0	2-1	5-0	1-2	2-0	1-1	0-0	2-0	2-0	■	1-0	1-0	2-1	0-1	1-0	2-1
Rushden & Diamonds	0-1	0-1	4-1	1-1	1-1	2-0	2-0	4-2	8-0	5-4	2-1	2-1	0-0	2-1	1-1	1-0	1-1	■	0-2	1-0	3-2	0-0	0-1
Salisbury City	0-2	4-1	3-0	2-1	2-2	1-1	3-1	1-3	0-1	2-0	3-1	3-0	2-0	1-0	1-1	0-1	1-1	1-3	■	0-1	1-0	1-1	1-0
Stevenage Borough	0-0	1-1	4-0	4-1	2-0	2-0	3-0	2-0	5-3	1-1	4-0	1-0	2-0	0-1	3-1	1-0	2-1	3-1	1-1	■	1-1	0-0	1-1
Tamworth	2-2	0-2	3-0	0-0	1-1	1-1	3-4	0-0	1-0	2-1	0-2	1-3	1-3	2-1	1-1	2-4	0-0	0-1	4-0	1-0	■	2-1	2-3
Wrexham	1-0	1-1	0-0	2-2	2-0	3-0	1-1	1-0	0-0	2-1	0-2	3-0	1-2	2-2	3-0	2-1	0-1	0-1	1-2	0-1	0-0	■	1-0
York City	5-0	2-1	3-0	2-2	2-0	0-1	1-0	2-0	1-0	1-1	4-1	3-1	2-0	3-2	0-0	3-0	1-1	0-0	1-2	1-1	1-1	2-1	■

Blue Square Premier (Football Conference)
Season 2009/2010

	P	W	D	L	F	A	Pts
Stevenage Borough	44	30	9	5	79	24	99
Luton Town	44	26	10	8	84	40	88
Oxford United	44	25	11	8	64	31	86
Rushden & Diamonds	44	22	13	9	77	39	79
York City	44	22	12	10	62	35	78
Kettering Town	44	18	12	14	51	41	66
Crawley Town	44	19	9	16	50	57	66
AFC Wimbledon	44	18	10	16	61	47	64
Mansfield Town	44	17	11	16	69	60	62
Cambridge United	44	15	14	15	65	53	59
Wrexham	44	15	13	16	45	39	58
Salisbury City	44	21	5	18	58	63	58
Kidderminster Harriers	44	15	12	17	57	52	57
Altrincham	44	13	15	16	53	51	54
Barrow	44	13	13	18	50	67	52
Tamworth	44	11	16	17	42	52	49
Hayes & Yeading United	44	12	12	20	59	85	48
Histon	44	11	13	20	44	67	46
Eastbourne Borough	44	11	13	20	42	72	46
Gateshead	44	13	7	24	46	69	45
Forest Green Rovers	44	12	9	23	50	76	45
Ebbsfleet United	44	12	7	25	49	82	43
Grays Athletic	44	5	13	26	35	91	26

Chester City were initially deducted 25 points for entering administration and insolvency but were then later expelled from the Conference and their record was expunged.
Salisbury City had 10 points deducted and were subsequently demoted from the Conference at the end of the season.
Grays Athletic had 2 points deducted and withdrew from the Conference at the end of the season.
Gateshead had 1 point deducted.

Promotion Play-offs

Rushden & Diamonds 1   Oxford United 1
York City 1   Luton Town 0

Oxford United 2   Rushden & Diamonds 0
Oxford United won 3-1 on aggregate.
Luton Town 0   York City 1
York City won 2-0 on aggregate

Oxford United 3   York City 1

Promoted: Stevenage Borough and Oxford United
Relegated: Ebbsfleet United and Grays Athletic

Blue Square North — 2009/2010 Season

	TEL	ALF	BLY	COR	DRO	EAS	FLE	GAI	GLO	HAR	HIN	HYD	ILK	NOR	RED	SOL	SOU	STA	STC	VAU	WOR
AFC Telford United	▓	2-0	1-1	2-4	1-2	1-1	0-0	2-2	0-1	2-1	2-2	4-0	0-0	1-2	3-0	0-0	0-2	2-1	0-1	5-1	1-0
Alfreton Town	4-0	▓	1-0	1-0	5-0	1-1	1-4	1-0	3-1	3-1	3-2	4-0	2-0	3-2	3-0	3-0	1-1	3-1	3-5	2-2	2-0
Blyth Spartans	4-0	2-0	▓	1-2	2-2	1-3	2-3	2-1	0-3	1-0	6-1	4-3	1-4	0-1	1-0	2-0	0-2	2-2	4-1	3-2	0-0
Corby Town	1-2	1-2	4-2	▓	1-0	1-1	0-2	2-2	3-6	3-0	1-1	2-0	2-2	1-0	2-2	1-2	1-1	3-2	5-1	4-1	0-2
Droylsden	1-5	0-0	2-1	1-2	▓	0-1	2-0	4-1	2-2	5-0	0-0	1-0	2-0	5-1	6-1	5-3	0-3	7-1	3-2	1-1	0-1
Eastwood Town	1-1	2-1	4-2	0-1	2-1	▓	0-1	1-0	0-3	1-0	1-0	2-0	0-3	1-1	3-1	2-1	0-3	0-0	1-3	0-0	1-2
Fleetwood Town	3-1	2-2	4-2	4-2	3-0	3-1	▓	2-2	3-1	2-2	3-1	1-1	1-0	0-3	8-0	3-0	4-0	2-1	2-0	4-2	4-0
Gainsborough Trinity	0-1	3-2	2-0	2-0	4-2	1-4	2-0	▓	1-0	1-1	1-1	2-1	0-0	1-4	3-0	0-0	2-4	1-3	1-3	2-0	0-1
Gloucester City	0-1	1-2	3-1	1-2	1-4	1-3	1-2	1-0	▓	0-1	3-5	2-0	0-1	0-1	2-0	1-0	2-2	2-0	1-2	1-0	0-2
Harrogate Town	0-3	0-4	2-5	0-4	2-2	0-1	0-1	2-0	1-1	▓	3-1	2-0	0-1	2-1	3-2	0-1	2-3	1-4	0-4	3-0	1-2
Hinckley Town	2-0	2-1	1-1	1-1	1-1	0-0	0-2	2-0	1-0	3-2	▓	1-2	1-0	5-1	0-3	4-1	3-1	0-0	1-1	1-2	
Hyde United	1-1	1-5	0-3	1-3	2-1	1-0	2-1	3-2	1-1	1-0	3-2	▓	1-1	1-1	3-2	1-1	1-1	1-0	2-1	2-2	0-2
Ilkeston Town	2-1	0-0	2-1	3-2	1-0	1-0	0-1	0-0	0-0	3-3	0-1	1-1	▓	1-1	3-2	1-0	3-2	2-3	3-2	4-0	1-3
Northwich Victoria	2-0	1-1	5-1	2-2	2-5	4-3	0-3	0-1	1-0	3-2	0-1	3-1	4-1	▓	0-2	2-0	1-1	2-2	2-1	0-0	2-3
Redditch United	3-1	3-0	2-2	1-0	1-3	1-2	0-0	0-3	4-1	2-0	0-2	0-0	2-2	1-1	▓	1-4	2-2	1-2	1-4	1-1	2-1
Solihull Moors	0-1	1-1	1-1	3-0	1-2	2-1	1-2	0-1	0-1	2-4	3-0	0-3	1-1	1-2		▓	1-1	1-1	2-2	4-0	1-2
Southport	3-0	1-3	3-2	4-0	3-3	5-1	5-0	0-0	3-2	3-1	1-1	4-1	1-1	2-1	2-0	3-0	▓	4-2	2-1	3-0	2-0
Stafford Rangers	2-0	1-1	1-1	0-2	2-2	3-3	2-2	2-1	1-0	1-0	2-3	1-1	0-1	2-2	0-1	2-3	1-2	▓	0-2	3-1	2-0
Stalybridge Celtic	0-3	0-1	0-1	1-3	2-2	1-0	2-3	3-2	4-1	3-0	0-0	2-4	1-0	1-1	3-0	4-1	0-1	2-2	▓	3-1	2-2
Vauxhall Motors	3-1	1-1	1-1	2-4	1-2	3-2	2-1	2-2	0-0	1-2	1-1	1-0	4-2	1-0	0-5	0-2	1-3	2-2	3-2	▓	1-1
Workington	2-1	1-1	3-1	1-1	0-1	1-0	1-0	1-1	2-0	1-1	0-1	2-2	0-0	0-1	1-0	1-0	0-2	1-1	1-0	1-0	▓

Blue Square North (Football Conference)

Season 2009/2010

Southport	40	25	11	4	91	45	86
Fleetwood Town	40	26	7	7	86	44	85
Alfreton Town	40	21	11	8	77	45	74
Workington	40	20	10	10	46	37	70
Droylsden	40	18	10	12	82	62	64
Corby Town	40	18	9	13	73	62	63
Hinckley United	40	16	14	10	60	52	62
Ilkeston Town	40	16	13	11	53	45	61
Stalybridge Celtic	40	16	7	17	71	64	55
Eastwood Town	40	15	9	16	50	55	54
AFC Telford United	40	14	9	17	52	55	51
Northwich Victoria	40	15	13	12	62	55	48
Blyth Spartans	40	13	9	18	67	72	48
Gainsborough Trinity	40	12	11	17	50	57	47
Hyde United	40	11	12	17	45	72	45
Stafford Rangers	40	10	14	16	59	70	44
Solihull Moors	40	11	9	20	47	58	42
Gloucester City	40	12	6	22	47	59	42
Redditch United	40	10	8	22	49	83	38
Vauxhall Motors	40	7	14	19	45	81	35
Harrogate Town	40	8	6	26	41	80	30

Farsley started the season with a 10 point deduction for entering administration. They later resigned from the Conference and their record was expunged.

Northwich Victoria were initially thrown out of the Conference for entering administration but, after a successful appeal, started the season with a 10 point deduction. They were subsequently demoted at the end of the season.

Promotion Play-offs North

Droylsden 2	Fleetwood Town 0
Workington 0	Alfreton Town 1

Fleetwood Town 3   Droylsden .... 1 (aet.)
Aggregate 3-3. Fleetwood Town won 4-3 on penalties
Alfreton Town 3   Workington 1
Alfreton Town won 4-1 on aggregate

Fleetwood Town 3   Alfreton Town 1

Promoted: Southport and Fleetwood Town
Relegated: None

Blue Square South 2009/2010 Season	Basingstoke Town	Bath City	Bishop's Stortford	Braintree Town	Bromley	Chelmsford City	Dorchester Town	Dover Athletic	Eastleigh	Hampton & Richmond Borough	Havant & Waterlooville	Lewes	Maidenhead United	Newport County	St. Albans City	Staines Town	Thurrock	Welling United	Weston-super-Mare	Weymouth	Woking	Worcester City
Basingstoke Town	■	1-0	0-2	0-1	2-3	2-1	2-1	1-3	0-1	1-2	1-1	1-1	0-0	1-5	1-1	0-1	0-4	1-1	2-1	2-1	1-2	0-1
Bath City	4-3	■	2-2	2-4	0-0	1-0	2-0	0-0	0-2	1-3	1-1	1-1	1-0	1-1	0-0	2-0	1-0	2-1	1-0	2-0	5-0	1-1
Bishop's Stortford	0-2	1-5	■	0-0	3-0	0-1	2-0	0-2	0-1	0-1	1-0	0-0	1-2	0-0	2-0	2-2	0-0	0-4	3-0	0-1	0-3	2-1
Braintree Town	1-2	2-0	2-0	■	1-1	2-1	2-0	1-2	1-1	1-1	0-2	3-0	2-0	1-2	2-2	3-1	1-0	1-0	3-2	1-0	0-0
Bromley	2-0	1-2	1-1	1-1	■	3-3	3-1	2-2	3-0	1-2	0-2	3-0	1-2	2-3	2-0	0-2	2-3	0-1	1-1	4-0	3-1	2-0
Chelmsford City	1-2	4-3	3-0	1-1	1-2	■	1-0	1-1	2-2	1-0	1-1	2-1	1-1	0-0	2-0	0-1	1-0	3-1	2-2	2-1	0-2	1-0
Dorchester Town	6-1	2-2	2-0	5-0	0-0	0-3	■	1-3	1-2	2-1	4-3	1-1	4-2	0-0	3-0	2-2	1-0	1-2	4-2	0-0	1-1	1-1
Dover Athletic	2-3	2-1	2-0	0-0	1-0	0-1	4-1	■	2-1	4-2	4-0	2-0	1-1	1-2	1-1	0-0	1-0	2-0	5-3	2-0	0-2	0-2
Eastleigh	6-0	1-1	1-1	1-2	6-1	3-1	2-0	1-2	■	0-0	0-1	1-0	0-3	1-4	0-1	0-0	2-8	1-3	3-1	4-0	0-2	4-1
Hampton & Richmond Borough	0-1	3-1	1-3	2-2	0-2	2-1	1-2	1-4	4-1	■	1-1	1-2	4-0	0-4	3-0	1-4	1-1	2-2	2-1	3-0	0-2	2-2
Havant & Waterlooville	0-2	2-2	2-1	1-1	2-1	5-2	0-1	2-1	2-2	1-1	■	1-1	1-0	4-0	0-1	1-0	1-1	2-2	6-0	3-1	1-1	3-2
Lewes	0-0	1-2	2-1	2-2	1-0	0-2	5-0	6-2	1-2	1-0	0-3	■	1-2	0-3	0-0	1-1	1-1	3-1	2-0	1-1	0-2	3-3
Maidenhead United	3-2	1-2	4-0	0-0	4-0	0-2	1-2	0-0	0-3	2-1	0-2	1-1	■	1-3	0-3	2-1	0-2	2-0	0-0	1-1	1-2	1-1
Newport County	1-0	1-0	1-0	1-0	2-0	4-0	3-0	3-0	5-1	3-1	2-0	2-2	4-1	■	5-0	1-0	5-0	2-2	2-0	1-1	1-0	1-0
St. Albans City	2-0	0-2	2-4	1-1	2-0	0-1	2-1	1-2	2-1	1-2	1-1	1-1	1-0	0-1	■	1-3	1-0	1-2	2-1	2-1	0-1	2-0
Staines Town	0-1	1-1	2-2	2-1	2-2	0-1	3-0	0-0	1-2	4-0	1-2	2-1	1-1	1-0	4-3	■	3-0	1-1	3-0	3-1	3-0	0-1
Thurrock	0-0	3-1	2-2	1-2	3-6	1-1	5-2	0-2	3-2	0-2	0-0	3-1	2-2	2-1	0-0	1-2	■	3-2	2-1	2-1	2-2	2-1
Welling United	1-1	0-2	0-2	0-0	0-2	0-1	1-1	0-1	1-2	2-0	1-0	1-0	3-1	0-2	3-2	3-0	2-2	■	3-1	7-1	1-2	1-0
Weston-super-Mare	1-1	0-2	1-3	1-2	3-3	1-2	0-2	3-1	2-2	1-1	1-2	3-2	1-4	1-4	2-3	0-1	1-3	1-2	■	3-0	1-1	3-1
Weymouth	0-6	0-2	2-6	1-1	1-5	1-4	2-0	1-2	0-5	1-0	0-1	3-1	0-5	1-3	0-2	1-2	0-0	0-3	1-2	■	0-0	2-1
Woking	4-2	1-3	1-0	0-0	2-1	1-2	3-1	2-0	1-0	3-1	2-0	1-1	0-1	0-1	0-0	0-1	0-1	0-5	2-1	4-0	■	1-0
Worcester City	1-1	0-2	1-1	2-3	1-2	1-2	4-0	1-0	4-1	0-1	0-2	1-2	1-0	1-4	0-0	0-0	1-2	0-1	4-1	3-1	3-2	■

Blue Square South (Football Conference)

Season 2009/2010

Newport County	42	32	7	3	93	26	103
Dover Athletic	42	22	9	11	66	47	75
Chelmsford City	42	22	9	11	62	48	75
Bath City	42	20	12	10	66	46	72
Woking	42	21	9	12	57	44	72
Havant & Waterlooville	42	19	14	9	65	44	71
Braintree Town	42	18	17	7	56	41	71
Staines Town	42	18	13	11	59	40	67
Welling United	42	18	9	15	66	51	63
Thurrock	42	16	13	13	66	60	61
Eastleigh	42	17	9	16	71	66	60
Bromley	42	15	10	17	68	64	55
St. Albans City	42	15	10	17	45	55	55
Hampton & Richmond Borough	42	14	9	19	56	66	51
Basingstoke Town	42	13	10	19	49	68	49
Maidenhead United	42	12	12	18	52	59	48
Dorchester Town	42	13	9	20	56	74	48
Bishop's Stortford	42	12	11	19	48	59	47
Lewes	42	9	15	18	49	63	42
Worcester City	42	10	10	22	48	60	40
Weston-super-Mare	42	5	8	29	48	93	23
Weymouth	42	5	7	30	31	103	22

Promotion Play-offs South

Woking .... 2 — Dover Athletic 1
Bath City .... 2 — Chelmsford City 0

Dover Athletic .... 0 — Woking 0
Woking won 2-1 on aggregate
Chelmsford City .... 0 — Bath City 1
Bath City won 3-0 on aggregate

Bath City .... 1 — Woking 0

Promoted: Newport County and Bath City
Relegated: Weston-super-Mare and Weymouth

Northern Premier League Premier Division 2009/2010 Season	Ashton United	Boston United	Bradford Park Avenue	Burscough	Buxton	Durham City	FC United of Manchester	Frickley Athletic	Guiseley	Hucknall Town	Kendal Town	Marine	Matlock Town	Nantwich Town	North Ferriby United	Ossett Town	Retford United	Stocksbridge Park Steels	Whitby Town	Worksop Town
Ashton United		0-2	3-2	1-1	1-2	1-0	2-2	1-3	3-2	1-2	2-3	0-2	0-2	3-2	0-1	2-0	1-0	0-1	2-2	2-1
Boston United	3-0		0-1	3-3	2-1	10-0	4-1	4-2	2-1	2-2	0-0	2-1	2-2	5-0	3-1	7-0	0-1	3-2	0-0	2-0
Bradford Park Avenue	0-1	2-2		1-3	0-0	7-1	3-2	3-1	2-4	2-0	3-2	2-0	5-2	3-2	1-2	4-2	0-1	2-0	1-0	1-0
Burscough	1-2	3-1	0-2		0-1	8-0	1-0	1-0	0-4	2-0	3-0	1-2	0-2	1-0	0-1	5-1	0-4	0-1	2-2	3-0
Buxton	2-0	0-1	1-1	2-2		6-2	3-0	4-1	3-1	2-0	1-2	2-2	1-1	0-0	1-1	2-2	0-2	3-1	0-2	1-0
Durham City	0-1	1-4	0-7	2-3	0-7		1-2	2-3	2-3	0-2	0-7	1-5	0-4	0-2	0-2	1-2	1-4	1-5	4-3	0-5
FC United of Manchester	2-3	1-2	1-5	2-0	0-1	1-2		0-0	1-2	2-0	1-4	3-0	1-0	4-0	3-3	1-1	2-4	4-3	1-1	2-0
Frickley Athletic	1-2	0-1	2-2	1-0	1-0	3-1	0-2		1-2	4-2	0-0	0-1	1-0	2-0	2-1	1-1	1-2	1-0	1-1	1-1
Guiseley	2-0	1-3	2-1	2-1	3-1	2-0	2-0	0-0		3-0	1-0	0-2	2-0	1-0	2-3	1-1	1-1	3-1	3-1	1-2
Hucknall Town	1-2	1-4	0-5	5-2	3-1	7-1	2-3	2-2	0-1		4-2	0-0	2-2	1-1	1-4	3-0	1-4	4-3	2-0	3-1
Kendal Town	0-0	1-0	1-1	3-2	0-2	5-0	1-0	3-1	2-1	3-1		4-1	1-1	1-2	2-0	2-2	2-1	1-1	2-0	4-1
Marine	3-4	0-0	1-3	2-1	1-1	7-2	1-1	2-0	0-1	2-1	4-3		2-1	0-2	1-3	2-0	1-2	2-1	2-0	1-1
Matlock Town	5-0	1-0	1-3	1-0	1-1	6-0	4-3	2-2	2-1	5-1	3-0	3-0		1-3	0-1	0-1	0-1	2-2	3-1	4-3
Nantwich Town	2-0	0-4	0-1	1-1	0-3	6-1	1-6	3-1	0-2	4-1	2-3	3-2	2-1		4-2	2-0	2-3	2-2	3-2	3-2
North Ferriby United	4-0	0-0	4-2	1-0	1-1	7-0	1-0	5-1	1-1	2-2	0-2	0-1	2-0	5-3		3-1	0-0	1-0	0-2	1-0
Ossett Town	0-3	0-5	4-6	1-2	3-1	3-0	1-2	4-1	1-4	2-2	3-2	1-4	0-1	0-1	0-1		1-2	2-4	1-3	0-2
Retford United	3-2	1-2	1-1	6-1	1-2	6-1	1-1	3-5	0-2	1-2	1-1	0-1	1-1	0-0	1-1	2-2		1-1	5-0	2-1
Stocksbridge Park Steels	2-1	2-1	2-3	4-1	3-1	6-0	1-1	4-1	2-4	2-3	0-2	4-2	3-4	5-3	1-1	3-1	1-2		2-0	2-2
Whitby Town	1-1	2-0	2-3	4-0	1-5	2-0	2-2	3-1	1-2	3-1	2-3	1-0	2-2	0-3	0-2	1-1	2-0	2-1		1-1
Worksop Town	1-1	1-5	1-3	0-1	1-1	4-0	3-1	1-2	1-3	1-1	0-1	1-0	0-3	0-0	0-2	3-1	3-3	1-2	0-4	

Unibond League Premier Division

Season 2009/2010

Guiseley	38	25	4	9	73	41	79
Bradford Park Avenue	38	24	6	8	94	51	78
Boston United	38	23	8	7	90	34	77
North Ferriby United	38	22	9	7	70	38	75
Kendal Town	38	21	8	9	75	47	71
Retford United	38	18	11	9	73	46	65
Matlock Town	38	17	9	12	72	49	60
Buxton	38	16	12	10	66	43	60
Marine	38	17	6	15	60	55	57
Nantwich Town	38	16	6	16	64	69	54
Stocksbridge Park Steels	38	15	7	16	80	68	52
Ashton United	38	15	6	17	48	63	51
FC United of Manchester	38	13	8	17	62	65	47
Whitby Town	38	12	10	16	56	62	46
Frickley Athletic	38	12	9	17	50	66	45
Burscough	38	13	5	20	55	65	44
Hucknall Town	38	12	8	18	65	81	44
Worksop Town	38	7	9	22	45	68	30
Ossett Town	38	6	7	25	46	92	25
Durham City	38	2	0	36	27	168	0

Durham City had 6 points deducted.

King's Lynn folded and their record was expunged.

Newcastle Blue Star folded and resigned from the League before the start of the season.

Promotion Play-offs

Bradford Park Avenue 2   Kendal Town 1

Boston United 2   North Ferriby United 1

Bradford Park Avenue 1   Boston United .... 2 (aet)

Promoted: Guiseley and Boston United

Relegated: Durham City

Southern Football League — Premier Division — 2009/2010 Season

	Banbury United	Bashley	Bedford Town	Brackley Town	Cambridge City	Chippenham Town	Clevedon Town	Didcot Town	Evesham United	Farnborough	Halesowen Town	Hednesford Town	Hemel Hempstead Town	Leamington	Merthyr Tydfil	Nuneaton Town	Oxford City	Rugby Town	Stourbridge	Swindon Supermarine	Tiverton Town	Truro City
Banbury United		1-1	0-0	0-3	1-0	0-0	4-3	1-0	0-1	0-3	2-1	3-2	1-1	1-2	3-1	2-1	1-1	2-1	3-3	3-1	0-1	0-0
Bashley	1-0		1-2	5-2	0-2	0-1	3-2	3-2	2-1	0-4	1-2	0-4	3-0	1-1	3-2	2-1	3-2	4-0	4-4	3-0	0-1	2-0
Bedford Town	1-1	0-4		2-2	0-2	1-2	3-1	1-5	1-2	2-2	1-1	3-2	5-0	0-2	2-4	2-1	1-1	3-1	0-1	1-2	2-0	0-2
Brackley Town	5-1	2-3	3-0		0-0	0-1	2-1	2-2	3-1	1-3	2-1	0-1	2-0	1-0	1-0	0-0	1-2	3-1	3-2	1-2	2-0	4-3
Cambridge City	2-1	2-2	4-2	5-0		1-0	4-1	4-1	1-1	1-1	1-1	0-3	1-1	2-2	1-1	1-1	2-0	1-0	6-1	5-0	1-1	0-3
Chippenham Town	5-0	1-2	3-0	2-3	2-1		2-0	2-0	2-1	2-0	1-1	0-1	6-1	4-2	1-5	2-1	2-0	1-0	2-2	0-1	4-2	2-1
Clevedon Town	1-2	0-2	0-3	0-3	0-1	0-0		1-1	1-4	1-4	3-3	0-3	1-0	1-3	1-1	0-3	1-2	1-3	4-1	2-6	0-1	0-3
Didcot Town	0-0	1-1	2-2	0-1	0-3	0-2	0-1		0-2	1-2	1-2	0-1	2-1	4-2	3-0	1-1	4-4	3-1	0-1	0-2	1-1	1-1
Evesham United	3-2	0-0	0-0	1-3	3-1	0-0	0-0	0-1		1-2	0-0	0-0	0-2	0-1	1-1	1-2	0-0	1-0	1-1	0-1	2-2	0-2
Farnborough	3-0	1-1	6-1	3-0	3-3	3-1	2-1	1-0	3-1		4-1	2-1	3-0	3-1	3-1	0-2	2-1	4-1	1-2	2-0	2-1	3-1
Halesowen Town	0-2	3-2	4-1	1-1	1-1	2-0	2-2	3-1	1-0	1-1		2-2	1-0	3-0	1-1	3-2	3-3	5-1	2-1	2-0	1-1	3-2
Hednesford Town	0-0	1-0	2-1	1-4	2-2	1-1	1-0	1-2	2-1	4-0	2-2		4-3	4-2	1-1	0-3	4-2	6-0	1-1	0-0	2-1	2-3
Hemel Hempstead Town	2-3	0-1	5-1	1-1	2-3	0-1	1-1	1-2	2-0	1-1	3-5	2-2		0-2	3-1	1-3	2-1	1-0	2-2	3-1	0-2	0-2
Leamington	3-3	0-1	2-0	2-1	1-0	4-4	0-1	3-5	4-1	2-3	2-2	1-3	3-1		5-3	0-2	1-2	2-1	2-1	3-1	5-0	1-3
Merthyr Tydfil	3-2	2-1	0-0	2-1	0-1	2-1	2-3	4-2	2-1	0-0	0-2	1-2	1-2	2-3		1-3	2-3	1-1	2-1	1-0	1-1	1-2
Nuneaton Town	5-0	5-2	4-0	2-2	1-1	0-1	4-2	2-0	2-0	1-1	1-1	3-1	3-1	1-1	3-1		3-1	1-1	0-0	1-0	1-0	4-0
Oxford City	1-1	1-1	4-1	2-3	0-1	0-0	1-2	1-1	3-0	1-1	2-2	2-0	2-2	1-1	2-2	1-4		3-0	1-3	2-1	1-0	2-2
Rugby Town	0-2	2-3	1-4	1-4	0-3	0-0	4-4	4-3	0-0	0-4	0-3	1-6	2-2	1-4	1-4	0-3	4-0		1-2	0-0	3-2	1-1
Stourbridge	2-1	2-2	2-0	4-2	3-1	1-0	4-1	1-0	0-0	3-2	1-4	1-1	2-0	2-1	2-0	1-2	0-2	6-0		0-0	2-1	7-2
Swindon Supermarine	1-2	3-3	0-0	1-7	1-1	1-1	3-2	1-1	1-1	0-7	1-2	0-0	1-0	2-3	1-1	2-4	2-4	5-1	2-2		2-1	0-4
Tiverton Town	2-1	0-5	2-0	1-1	0-0	0-0	0-0	1-2	0-1	0-2	0-2	0-2	0-0	2-3	0-1	1-2	1-0	3-1	2-2	0-0		1-2
Truro City	1-1	1-1	5-1	1-1	1-1	3-5	2-2	2-1	1-2	2-3	1-2	1-2	3-1	2-2	3-1	0-2	0-1	4-1	4-1	0-0	2-0	

Southern League Premier Division

Season 2009/2010

	P	W	D	L	F	A	Pts
Farnborough	42	28	9	5	100	44	93
Nuneaton Town	42	26	10	6	91	37	88
Chippenham Town	42	21	11	10	67	43	74
Hednesford Town	42	20	13	9	79	51	73
Brackley Town	42	21	9	12	83	61	72
Cambridge City	42	18	17	7	73	44	71
Bashley	42	20	11	11	79	61	71
Halesowen Town	42	21	17	4	84	53	70
Stourbridge	42	19	13	10	80	65	70
Leamington	42	19	8	15	84	75	65
Truro City	42	17	11	14	78	65	62
Banbury United	42	14	13	15	53	67	55
Oxford City	42	13	15	14	63	66	54
Swindon Supermarine	42	10	14	18	48	76	44
Didcot Town	42	10	11	21	56	70	41
Evesham United	42	9	14	19	35	52	41
Merthyr Tydfil	42	12	11	19	62	72	37
Bedford Town	42	9	10	23	50	88	37
Tiverton Town	42	8	12	22	35	61	36
Hemel Hempstead Town	42	8	10	24	50	81	34
Clevedon Town	42	6	11	25	48	92	29
Rugby Town	42	4	8	30	41	114	20

Halesowen Town and Merthyr Tydfil both had 10 points deducted for entering administration.

Promotion Play-offs

Chippenham Town 2   Hednesford Town 0

Nuneaton Town 6   Brackley Town 0

Nuneaton Town 2   Chippenham Town .... 1 (aet)

Promoted: Farnborough and Nuneaton Town

Relegated: Hemel Hempstead Town, Clevedon Town and Rugby Town

80

Isthmian Football League Premier Division 2009/2010 Season

Home \ Away	AFC Hornchurch	Ashford Town (Middlesex)	Aveley	Billericay Town	Bognor Regis Town	Boreham Wood	Canvey Island	Carshalton Athletic	Cray Wanderers	Dartford	Harrow Borough	Hastings United	Hendon	Horsham	Kingstonian	Maidstone United	Margate	Sutton United	Tonbridge Angels	Tooting & Mitcham United	Waltham Abbey	Wealdstone
AFC Hornchurch		1-0	2-1	0-0	3-0	2-1	1-0	2-2	0-2	0-2	2-1	1-1	4-4	2-1	1-1	1-0	1-0	1-0	1-1	0-1	4-1	0-0
Ashford Town (Middlesex)	1-1		2-2	3-2	2-2	0-2	1-1	1-2	3-0	1-4	2-6	3-2	1-1	0-2	3-1	0-2	2-2	0-1	3-2	2-1	1-1	3-3
Aveley	1-1	2-1		1-0	2-0	2-0	4-2	4-0	1-1	1-4	1-2	3-0	1-2	2-1	3-4	2-0	0-3	0-1	2-0	1-2	3-1	2-2
Billericay Town	2-0	0-1	2-1		1-0	2-0	4-1	0-4	1-1	1-0	1-2	2-0	1-0	1-2	1-5	1-1	1-2	0-1	1-1	0-0	1-1	0-0
Bognor Regis Town	4-2	2-0	1-1	1-1		0-1	2-2	1-0	1-1	0-2	1-1	0-3	1-1	3-1	3-0	3-3	1-2	3-1	0-3	1-2		2-2
Boreham Wood	0-0	3-3	3-2	2-0	1-0		1-3	3-1	2-4	0-1	1-0	0-0	2-1	4-0	0-1	0-2	1-1	1-2	2-0	3-2	3-0	0-1
Canvey Island	1-0	2-1	1-4	0-0	0-0	0-1		2-2	5-1	2-5	1-1	1-0	2-3	1-2	1-2	0-1	2-0	1-2	1-1	2-1	2-3	1-1
Carshalton Athletic	1-0	3-1	0-3	1-0	1-0	0-0	0-0		2-0	0-4	2-2	1-3	0-0	1-2	1-2	1-2	0-0	1-2	4-1	4-1	4-2	
Cray Wanderers	1-0	1-0	1-2	0-2	0-2	1-1	1-2	3-3		1-2	1-3	1-2	2-0	1-1	2-1	1-0	3-2	1-2	1-3	1-0	1-2	1-3
Dartford	0-1	3-2	2-2	1-4	3-3	1-2	2-1	1-1	1-1		2-0	4-3	5-0	3-2	5-0	3-0	0-1	0-2	2-0	3-2	2-1	1-1
Harrow Borough	0-0	1-2	3-3	1-0	1-2	2-0	0-0	3-3	1-1	0-1		0-3	0-3	2-2	2-0	2-1	3-0	1-1	1-3	1-1	5-3	3-1
Hastings United	1-0	4-4	0-1	1-1	1-2	2-1	1-1	3-1	2-3	1-3	1-1		2-1	3-1	0-0	1-2	2-1	1-3	5-1	2-0	2-0	1-0
Hendon	3-2	2-1	4-1	1-0	2-0	0-1	2-1	1-0	2-0	1-2	3-1	1-3		1-1	0-3	3-0	1-2	1-2	0-0	0-0	0-2	2-3
Horsham	2-1	4-1	0-2	0-2	2-1	1-3	1-2	2-2	4-0	1-3	2-0	4-2	3-1		0-1	1-0	3-3	1-0	0-3	1-2	2-1	1-3
Kingstonian	2-0	1-0	1-6	2-1	1-3	4-1	1-0	4-1	2-6	3-5	1-2	3-0	2-1			1-1	2-0	2-1	2-3	1-1	1-1	3-3
Maidstone United	0-0	2-0	4-2	1-0	1-0	0-1	0-3	0-2	1-1	0-1	0-3	0-5	0-3	1-1	1-3		0-1	2-1	2-2	1-2	2-0	2-3
Margate	0-0	1-1	2-3	1-3	1-1	2-1	1-2	1-1	0-1	0-4	2-2	1-0	2-3	1-3	2-1	0-1		1-1	0-3	2-1	0-3	1-1
Sutton United	4-1	2-4	3-2	2-1	0-0	0-1	1-2	3-0	1-4	0-3	1-0	2-2	3-1	2-1	1-1	0-0	4-0		2-1	1-2	0-0	5-0
Tonbridge Angels	1-2	3-2	3-2	0-1	2-0	0-2	3-1	2-0	3-2	1-4	3-2	2-2	1-2	1-0	2-1	0-0	1-2			1-2	2-0	2-3
Tooting & Mitcham United	2-3	2-3	1-2	1-1	3-1	0-2	1-3	2-2	0-2	3-1	1-0	1-0	0-2	0-2	2-3	2-2	2-1	1-1	5-3		1-1	3-2
Waltham Abbey	0-5	0-1	0-2	0-2	4-1	1-1	2-1	2-1	0-1	0-4	1-1	0-1	1-0	2-1	1-0	1-2	3-4	1-2	0-2	1-1		1-2
Wealdstone	2-3	1-0	0-1	0-0	4-0	0-0	1-0	1-4	3-2	1-1	2-1	1-0	0-2	2-1	2-2	2-2	1-0	2-1	2-1	0-2	2-4	

Rymans League Premier Division

Season 2009/2010

Team	P	W	D	L	F	A	Pts
Dartford	42	29	6	7	101	45	93
Sutton United	42	22	9	11	65	45	75
Aveley	42	21	7	14	83	62	70
Boreham Wood	42	20	8	14	54	44	68
Kingstonian	42	20	8	14	73	69	68
Wealdstone	42	17	14	11	65	65	65
Hastings United	42	18	9	15	68	56	63
Tonbridge Angels	42	18	8	16	69	67	62
AFC Hornchurch	42	16	13	13	51	47	61
Hendon	42	18	6	18	61	59	60
Horsham	42	16	8	18	65	67	56
Tooting & Mitcham United	42	15	10	17	60	64	55
Billericay Town	42	14	12	16	44	42	54
Harrow Borough	42	13	14	15	66	63	53
Cray Wanderers	42	14	9	19	54	70	51
Canvey Island	42	13	11	18	57	62	50
Carshalton Athletic	42	12	13	17	58	64	49
Maidstone United	42	13	10	19	39	57	49
Margate	42	11	12	19	50	72	45
Ashford Town (Middlesex)	42	11	11	20	62	80	44
Waltham Abbey	42	12	8	22	49	74	44
Bognor Regis Town	42	9	14	19	45	65	41

Promotion Play-offs

Aveley 0   Boreham Wood 1
Sutton United 2   Kingstonian 4

Boreham Wood 2   Kingstonian 0

Promoted: Dartford and Boreham Wood

Relegated: Ashford Town (Middlesex), Waltham Abbey and Bognor Regis Town

F.A. Trophy 2009/2010

Qualifying 1	AFC Hornchurch	2	Brentwood Town	1	
Qualifying 1	AFC Sudbury	3	Billericay Town	3	
Qualifying 1	AFC Totton	2	Woodford United	2	
Qualifying 1	Ashton United	1	FC United of Manchester	3	
Qualifying 1	Atherstone Town	1	Leigh Genesis	3	
Qualifying 1	Aveley	2	Carshalton Athletic	5	
Qualifying 1	Banbury United	2	Bridgwater Town	2	
Qualifying 1	Beaconsfield SYCOB	1	Bashley	4	
Qualifying 1	Biggleswade Town	2	Chipstead	2	
Qualifying 1	Billericay Town	2	AFC Sudbury	2	(aet)
	Billericay Town won on penalties				
Qualifying 1	Bognor Regis Town	3	Ashford Town	1	
Qualifying 1	Boston United	3	Chorley	2	
Qualifying 1	Bracknell Town	1	Thatcham Town	8	
Qualifying 1	Bradford Park Avenue	0	Clitheroe	1	
Qualifying 1	Brigg Town	3	Burscough	2	
Qualifying 1	Burnham	3	Cinderford Town	2	
Qualifying 1	Buxton	1	Hednesford Town	0	
Qualifying 1	Cammell Laird	0	Guiseley	3	
Qualifying 1	Canvey Island	1	Hitchin Town	2	
Qualifying 1	Chesham United	2	Oxford City	2	
Qualifying 1	Chippenham Town	3	Frome Town	1	
Qualifying 1	Chipstead	2	Biggleswade Town	2	(aet)
	Chipstead won on penalties				
Qualifying 1	Cirencester Town	1	Godalming Town	3	
Qualifying 1	Clevedon Town	2	Brackley Town	4	
Qualifying 1	Corinthian Casuals	0	Arlesey Town	3	
Qualifying 1	Cray Wanderers	1	Burgess Hill Town	2	
Qualifying 1	Croydon Athletic	2	Ashford Town (Middlesex)	1	
Qualifying 1	Didcot Town	0	Cambridge City	1	
Qualifying 1	Evesham United	1	Windsor & Eton	1	
Qualifying 1	FC Halifax Town	2	Romulus	0	
Qualifying 1	Frickley Athletic	2	Bamber Bridge	1	
Qualifying 1	Garforth Town	0	AFC Fylde	3	
Qualifying 1	Hastings United	1	Merstham	6	
Qualifying 1	Hemel Hempstead Town	0	Farnborough	1	
Qualifying 1	Hendon	2	Lowestoft Town	0	
Qualifying 1	Horsham	4	Barton Rovers	4	
Qualifying 1	Hungerford Town	4	Taunton Town	3	
Qualifying 1	Lancaster City	1	Chasetown	1	
Qualifying 1	Leamington	1	Stourbridge	2	
Qualifying 1	Leek Town	2	Kendal Town	1	
Qualifying 1	Leighton Town	0	Whyteleafe	3	
Qualifying 1	Marine	0	King's Lynn	1	
Qualifying 1	Matlock Town	2	Loughborough Dynamo	1	
Qualifying 1	Merthyr Tydfil	0	Marlow	0	
Qualifying 1	Metropolitan Police	0	Kingstonian	1	
Qualifying 1	North Ferriby United	1	Worksop Town	1	
Qualifying 1	Northwood	1	Abingdon United	0	
Qualifying 1	Nuneaton Town	1	Hucknall Town	1	
Qualifying 1	Ossett Town	1	Willenhall Town	2	
Qualifying 1	Radcliffe Borough	2	Quorn	2	
Qualifying 1	Ramsgate	3	Leatherhead	0	
Qualifying 1	Retford United	0	Nantwich Town	1	

Qualifying 1	Rugby Town	0	Gosport Borough	1	
Qualifying 1	Rushall Olympic	0	Carlton Town	1	
Qualifying 1	Salford City	3	Durham City	0	
Qualifying 1	Shepshed Dynamo	2	Harrogate Railway Athletic	1	
Qualifying 1	Sittingbourne	0	Dartford	1	
Qualifying 1	Skelmersdale United	5	Goole AFC	0	
Qualifying 1	Soham Town Rangers	2	Harrow Borough	2	
Qualifying 1	Spalding United	1	Mossley	3	
Qualifying 1	Stocksbridge Park Steels	1	Glapwell	2	
Qualifying 1	Sutton United	0	Tonbridge Angels	2	
Qualifying 1	Swindon Supermarine	2	Fleet Town	4	
Qualifying 1	Tiverton Town	0	Truro City	4	
Qualifying 1	Tooting & Mitcham United	3	Walton & Hersham	0	
Qualifying 1	Uxbridge	1	Slough Town	1	
Qualifying 1	VCD Athletic	0	Concord Rangers	1	
Qualifying 1	Waltham Abbey	0	Boreham Wood	2	
Qualifying 1	Waltham Forest	1	Maidstone United	1	
Qualifying 1	Ware	1	Enfield Town	3	
Qualifying 1	Wealdstone	3	Margate	1	
Qualifying 1	Whitby Town	5	Warrington Town	2	
Qualifying 1	Witton Albion	1	Sutton Coldfield Town	1	
Qualifying 1	Yate Town	2	Bedford Town	1	
Replay	Barton Rovers	4	Horsham	3	
Replay	Bridgwater Town	0	Banbury United	1	
Replay	Chasetown	1	Lancaster City	4	
Replay	Harrow Borough	5	Soham Town Rangers	1	
Replay	Hucknall Town	0	Nuneaton Town	3	
Replay	Maidstone United	1	Waltham Forest	0	
Replay	Marlow	4	Merthyr Tydfil	2	
Replay	Oxford City	2	Chesham United	0	
Replay	Quorn	6	Radcliffe Borough	3	
Replay	Slough Town	2	Uxbridge	0	
Replay	Sutton Coldfield Town	2	Witton Albion	3	(aet)
Replay	Windsor & Eton	0	Evesham United	2	
Replay	Woodford United	1	AFC Totton	4	
Replay	Worksop Town	4	North Ferriby United	4	(aet)
	North Ferriby United won on penalties				
Qualifying 2	AFC Fylde	2	Glapwell	1	
Qualifying 2	Arlesey Town	2	Oxford City	1	
Qualifying 2	Barton Rovers	2	Billericay Town	2	
Qualifying 2	Bashley	2	Marlow	1	
Qualifying 2	Bognor Regis Town	0	Maidstone United	2	
Qualifying 2	Boreham Wood	3	Slough Town	2	
Qualifying 2	Boston United	0	Quorn	0	
Qualifying 2	Brackley Town	1	Mossley	1	
Qualifying 2	Buxton	0	Stourbridge	1	
Qualifying 2	Cambridge City	0	Matlock Town	1	
Qualifying 2	Carlton Town	0	North Ferriby United	3	
Qualifying 2	Carshalton Athletic	3	AFC Totton	1	
Qualifying 2	Chippenham Town	4	Tooting & Mitcham United	1	
Qualifying 2	Concord Rangers	2	Enfield Town	0	
Qualifying 2	Croydon Athletic	1	Burnham	1	
Qualifying 2	Dartford	3	Chipstead	0	
Qualifying 2	Farnborough	5	Burgess Hill Town	2	
Qualifying 2	Fleet Town	0	Ramsgate	2	
Qualifying 2	Frickley Athletic	0	Guiseley	3	

Qualifying 2	Godalming Town	1	Banbury United	1	
Qualifying 2	Harrow Borough	2	Wealdstone	2	
Qualifying 2	Hitchin Town	3	Gosport Borough	1	
Qualifying 2	Kingstonian	4	Hendon	2	
Qualifying 2	Lancaster City	3	FC United of Manchester	3	
Qualifying 2	Leigh Genesis	4	Skelmersdale United	1	
Qualifying 2	Nantwich Town	4	Leek Town	1	
Qualifying 2	Northwood	0	Evesham United	0	
Qualifying 2	Salford City	5	Clitheroe	3	
Qualifying 2	Shepshed Dynamo	0	FC Halifax Town	5	
Qualifying 2	Tonbridge Angels	6	Merstham	1	
Qualifying 2	Truro City	4	Thatcham Town	1	
Qualifying 2	Whitby Town	0	King's Lynn	2	
Qualifying 2	Whyteleafe	1	AFC Hornchurch	1	
Qualifying 2	Willenhall Town	0	Nuneaton Town	6	
Qualifying 2	Witton Albion	4	Brigg Town	1	
Qualifying 2	Yate Town	1	Hungerford Town	1	
Replay	AFC Hornchurch	4	Whyteleafe	0	
Replay	Banbury United	1	Godalming Town	3	
Replay	Billericay Town	3	Barton Rovers	0	
Replay	Burnham	2	Croydon Athletic	1	
Replay	Evesham United	1	Northwood	2	
Replay	FC United of Manchester	1	Lancaster City	0	(aet)
Replay	Hungerford Town	3	Yate Town	0	
Replay	Mossley	3	Brackley Town	1	(aet)
Replay	Quorn	3	Boston United	2	
Replay	Wealdstone	2	Harrow Borough	1	
Qualifying 3	AFC Fylde	1	Hinckley United	1	
Qualifying 3	Bashley	2	Staines Town	1	
Qualifying 3	Billericay Town	0	Hitchin Town	0	
Qualifying 3	Blyth Spartans	2	Stafford Rangers	0	
Qualifying 3	Boreham Wood	1	Hungerford Town	0	
Qualifying 3	Bromley	0	Maidstone United	1	
Qualifying 3	Chelmsford City	4	AFC Hornchurch	4	
Qualifying 3	Corby Town	1	Alfreton Town	1	
Qualifying 3	Dover Athletic	3	Dartford	2	
Qualifying 3	Eastleigh	1	Lewes	1	
Qualifying 3	Eastwood Town	0	Nantwich Town	3	
Qualifying 3	FC United of Manchester	2	Harrogate Town	2	
Qualifying 3	Farnborough	3	Wealdstone	0	
Qualifying 3	Farsley Celtic	5	Droylsden	2	
Qualifying 3	Fleetwood Town	2	Northwich Victoria	0	
Qualifying 3	Godalming Town	0	Arlesey Town	3	
Qualifying 3	Guiseley	3	FC Halifax Town	1	
Qualifying 3	Hampton & Richmond Borough	3	Concord Rangers	2	
Qualifying 3	Hyde United	3	Nuneaton Town	3	
Qualifying 3	Ilkeston Town	1	Mossley	1	
Qualifying 3	King's Lynn	1	Salford City	0	
Qualifying 3	Kingstonian	0	Chippenham Town	2	
Qualifying 3	Leigh Genesis	0	Redditch United	1	
Qualifying 3	Maidenhead United	1	Bath City	0	
Qualifying 3	Newport County	2	Braintree Town	1	
Qualifying 3	North Ferriby United	2	Gainsborough Trinity	2	
Qualifying 3	Northwood	2	Basingstoke Town	1	
Qualifying 3	Quorn	2	Vauxhall Motors (Cheshire)	3	
Qualifying 3	Ramsgate	0	Bishop's Stortford	3	

Qualifying 3	Stalybridge Celtic	1	AFC Telford United	1	
Qualifying 3	Stourbridge	0	Southport	0	
Qualifying 3	Thurrock	1	Havant & Waterlooville	4	
Qualifying 3	Truro City	1	Gloucester City	0	
Qualifying 3	Welling United	3	Tonbridge Angels	2	
Qualifying 3	Weston Super Mare	1	Carshalton Athletic	1	
Qualifying 3	Weymouth	3	Dorchester Town	0	
Qualifying 3	Witton Albion	1	Matlock Town	1	
Qualifying 3	Woking	6	St Albans City	0	
Qualifying 3	Worcester City	2	Burnham	1	
Qualifying 3	Workington	1	Solihull Moors	1	
Replay	AFC Hornchurch	1	Chelmsford City	2	
Replay	AFC Telford United	1	Stalybridge Celtic	2	
Replay	Alfreton Town	1	Corby Town	2	(aet)
Replay	Carshalton Athletic	3	Weston Super Mare	1	
Replay	Gainsborough Trinity	3	North Ferriby United	3	(aet)
	Gainsborough Trinity won on penalties				
Replay	Hinckley United	7	AFC Fylde	3	
Replay	Hitchin Town	0	Billericay Town	1	
Replay	Lewes	1	Eastleigh	0	
Replay	Matlock Town	4	Witton Albion	3	(aet)
Replay	Mossley	0	Ilkeston Town	2	
Replay	Nuneaton Town	1	Hyde United	0	
Replay	Solihull Moors	2	Workington	4	
Replay	Southport	4	Stourbridge	2	
Round 1	AFC Wimbledon	2	Boreham Wood	1	
Round 1	Arlesey Town	1	Chippenham Town	1	
Round 1	Bashley	2	Crawley Town	3	
Round 1	Bishop's Stortford	1	Maidenhead United	2	
Round 1	Blyth Spartans	2	Ilkeston Town	0	
Round 1	Cambridge United	3	Luton Town	1	
Round 1	Carshalton Athletic	1	Northwood	1	
Round 1	Chelmsford City	2	Truro City	2	
Round 1	Chester City	0	Fleetwood Town	1	
Round 1	Corby Town	2	Farsley Celtic	0	
Round 1	Farnborough	1	Newport County	3	
Round 1	Gateshead	1	Harrogate Town	1	
Round 1	Guiseley	1	Redditch United	0	
Round 1	Hampton & Richmond Borough	0	Lewes	0	
Round 1	Havant & Waterlooville	2	Dover Athletic	3	
Round 1	Hinckley United	0	York City	0	
Round 1	Kettering Town	0	Barrow	1	
Round 1	Maidstone United	0	Histon	3	
	Maidstone United progressed to Round 2 after Histon were disqualified for fielding an ineligible player.				
Round 1	Mansfield Town	0	Tamworth	2	
Round 1	Matlock Town	0	Kidderminster Harriers	2	
Round 1	Nantwich Town	0	Stalybridge Celtic	3	
Round 1	Oxford United	1	Hayes & Yeading United	0	
Round 1	Rushden & Diamonds	1	Billericay Town	0	
Round 1	Southport	2	Gainsborough Trinity	2	
Round 1	Stevenage Borough	2	Ebbsfleet United	0	
Round 1	Vauxhall Motors (Cheshire)	8	King's Lynn	0	
Round 1	Welling United	0	Eastbourne Borough	1	
Round 1	Weymouth	0	Salisbury City	1	
Round 1	Woking	1	Forest Green Rovers	0	
Round 1	Worcester City	3	Grays Athletic	1	
Round 1	Workington	2	Nuneaton Town	1	
Round 1	Wrexham	0	Altrincham	0	

Replay	Altrincham	1	Wrexham	0
Replay	Chippenham Town	2	Arlesey Town	0
Replay	Gainsborough Trinity	1	Southport	0
Replay	Harrogate Town	0	Gateshead	2
Replay	Lewes	3	Hampton & Richmond Borough	1
Replay	Northwood	0	Carshalton Athletic	5
Replay	Truro City	0	Chelmsford City	1
Replay	York City	3	Hinckley United	1
Round 2	AFC Wimbledon	3	Altrincham	1
Round 2	Blyth Spartans	1	Guiseley	2
Round 2	Cambridge United	2	Eastbourne Borough	2
Round 2	Chelmsford City	2	Crawley Town	1
Round 2	Fleetwood Town	0	Dover Athletic	1
Round 2	Gainsborough Trinity	0	Tamworth	0
Round 2	Gateshead	1	Chippenham Town	0
Round 2	Kidderminster Harriers	3	Lewes	2
Round 2	Maidenhead United	0	Barrow	1
Round 2	Newport County	0	York City	0
Round 2	Oxford United	1	Woking	0
Round 2	Salisbury City	2	Maidstone United	0
Round 2	Stalybridge Celtic	1	Corby Town	2
Round 2	Stevenage Borough	6	Vauxhall Motors (Cheshire)	0
Round 2	Worcester City	1	Carshalton Athletic	1
Round 2	Workington	2	Rushden & Diamonds	1
Replay	Carshalton Athletic	0	Worcester City	4
Replay	Eastbourne Borough	0	Cambridge United	2
Replay	Tamworth	2	Gainsborough Trinity	1
Replay	York City	1	Newport County	0
Round 3	AFC Wimbledon	2	Workington	3
Round 3	Barrow	1	Gateshead	1
Round 3	Cambridge United	0	Salisbury City	0
Round 3	Chelmsford City	1	Oxford United	3
Round 3	Guiseley	0	Tamworth	1
Round 3	Stevenage Borough	4	Dover Athletic	1
Round 3	Worcester City	0	Kidderminster Harriers	1
Round 3	York City	1	Corby Town	0
Replay	Gateshead	2	Barrow	3
Replay	Salisbury City	2	Cambridge United	1
Round 4	Barrow	2	York City	1
Round 4	Oxford United	1	Kidderminster Harriers	2
Round 4	Salisbury City	2	Tamworth	1
Round 4	Stevenage Borough	2	Workington	1
Semi-finals				
1st leg	Kidderminster Harriers	1	Stevenage Borough	5
2nd leg	Stevenage Borough	0	Kidderminster Harriers	0
	Stevenage Borough won 5-1 on aggregate			
1st leg	Salisbury City	0	Barrow	1
2nd leg	Barrow	2	Salisbury City	1
	Barrow won 3-1 on aggregate			
FINAL	Barrow	2	Stevenage Borough	1

86

F.A. Vase 2009/2010

Round 1	AFC Wulfrunians	1	Friar Lane & Epworth	5	
Round 1	Almondsbury Town	3	Melksham Town	1	
Round 1	Ardley United	0	Moneyfields	1	
Round 1	Armthorpe Welfare	3	Liversedge	1	
Round 1	Arnold Town	0	Long Eaton United	1	
Round 1	Ash United	3	Badshot Lea	4	(aet)
Round 1	Bartley Green	1	Newcastle Town	2	(aet)
Round 1	Bedfont	1	Shoreham	1	(aet)
Round 1	Bemerton Heath Harlequins	1	Alresford Town	1	(aet)
Round 1	Bewdley Town	2	Coleshill Town	1	
Round 1	Biddulph Victoria	2	Norton United	1	
Round 1	Biggleswade United	2	Kingsbury London Tigers	1	
Round 1	Blaby & Whetstone Athletic	3	Malvern Town	1	
Round 1	Blackstones	1	Lincoln Moorlands Railway	2	
Round 1	Bodmin Town	1	Saltash United	2	
Round 1	Borrowash Victoria	0	Gedling Town	4	
Round 1	Bottesford Town	0	Ollerton Town	1	
Round 1	Bourne Town	0	New Mills	1	
	A replay was ordered after New Mills were found to have fielded an ineligible player.				
Round 1	Bridlington Town	2	South Shields	0	
Round 1	Brislington	8	Porthleven	0	
Round 1	Bristol Manor Farm	2	Corsham Town	1	
Round 1	Broxbourne Borough V&E	1	Stotfold	2	
Round 1	Burnham Ramblers	1	Bedford	2	
Round 1	Cambridge Regional College	7	March Town United	1	
Round 1	Cheadle Town	2	Congleton Town	2	(aet)
Round 1	Clevedon United	3	Tavistock	5	
Round 1	Cockfosters	1	North Greenford United	2	
Round 1	Colne	0	Hallam	4	
Round 1	Consett	0	Bedlington Terriers	2	
Round 1	Crook Town	2	Northallerton Town	0	
Round 1	Daisy Hill	6	Worsbrough Bridge Athletic	2	
Round 1	Daventry Town	2	Rothwell Corinthians	0	
Round 1	Daventry United	2	Wellingborough Town	3	(aet)
Round 1	Dawlish Town	3	Liskeard Athletic	0	
Round 1	Dorking	0	Chertsey Town	2	
Round 1	Downton	2	Fareham Town	4	(aet)
Round 1	Dunkirk	2	Winterton Rangers	0	(aet)
Round 1	East Grinstead Town	0	Whitehawk	5	
Round 1	Eastbourne United	4	Greenwich Borough	3	(aet)
Round 1	Ely City	3	Eynesbury Rovers	2	
Round 1	Enfield 1893	1	Southend Manor	0	
Round 1	Epsom & Ewell	3	Farnborough North End	2	(aet)
Round 1	Erith & Belvedere	2	Pagham	1	
Round 1	Felixstowe & Walton United	1	Long Buckby	1	(aet)
Round 1	Grimsby Borough	1	Gresley	3	
Round 1	Guisborough Town	1	Norton & Stockton Ancients	2	
Round 1	Halstead Town	3	Dunstable Town	0	
Round 1	Haverhill Rovers	2	Bugbrooke St Michaels	3	
Round 1	Herne Bay	1	Hythe Town	0	
Round 1	Hillingdon Borough	1	Brimsdown Rovers	2	
Round 1	Kidlington	1	Bradford Town	2	
Round 1	Kirkley & Pakefield	3	Newmarket Town	1	
Round 1	Langford	1	Wembley	2	
Round 1	Laverstock & Ford	1	Brockenhurst	2	

Round 1	Leeds Carnegie	2	Shildon	3	
Round 1	Leverstock Green	0	Hadley	1	
Round 1	London Colney	2	Bethnal Green United	1	
Round 1	Longwell Green Sports	2	Wantage Town	1	
Round 1	Loughborough University	1	Causeway United	1	(aet)
Round 1	Louth Town	3	Sleaford Town	4	(aet)
Round 1	Mole Valley SCR	0	Beckenham Town	1	
Round 1	Molesey	1	Arundel	2	
Round 1	Nelson	2	Selby Town	0	
Round 1	Newcastle Benfield	1	Tow Law Town	0	
Round 1	Newport Pagnell Town	5	Erith Town	1	
Round 1	North Shields	2	Pickering Town	3	
Round 1	Northampton Spencer	0	Wroxham	3	
Round 1	Oldham Town	0	Winsford United	1	
Round 1	Padiham	4	Hemsworth MW	2	
Round 1	Peacehaven & Telscombe	3	Chichester City	1	
Round 1	Penrith	5	Dinnington Town	0	
Round 1	Plymouth Parkway	4	St Blazey	2	(aet)
Round 1	Poole Town	4	Bishop Sutton	1	
Round 1	Rainworth MW	2	Deeping Rangers	1	
Round 1	Ramsbottom United	2	Bacup Borough	4	(aet)
Round 1	Redhill	3	Camberley Town	1	(aet)
Round 1	Ringmer	2	Crowborough Athletic	3	
Round 1	Rossington Main	0	Alsager Town	3	
Round 1	Royston Town	5	Basildon United	3	
Round 1	Shortwood United	3	Winchester City	1	
Round 1	Shrivenham	0	Flackwell Heath	2	
Round 1	Southam United	1	Oadby Town	2	(aet)
Round 1	Stokesley SC	0	Morpeth Town	2	
Round 1	Studley	0	Boldmere St Michaels	1	
Round 1	Tipton Town	3	Kirby Muxloe	1	
Round 1	Tiptree United	1	Harefield United	0	(aet)
Round 1	Tividale	3	Wolverhampton Casuals	2	(aet)
Round 1	United Services Portsmouth	0	Hamble ASSC	1	
Round 1	Walsall Wood	0	Westfields	2	
Round 1	Wednesfield	0	Barwell	3	
Round 1	Wellington	4	Dosthill Colts	1	
Round 1	Wellington Town	3	Barnstaple Town	1	
Round 1	Wells City	3	Verwood Town	0	
Round 1	Welton Rovers	6	Keynsham Town	0	
Round 1	West Auckland Town	5	Hall Road Rangers	1	
Round 1	Westbury United	0	Carterton	1	
Round 1	Whickham	1	Tadcaster Albion	0	(aet)
Round 1	Whitton United	1	Woodbridge Town	3	
Round 1	Wick	1	Faversham Town	2	
Round 1	Willand Rovers	5	Newquay	2	
Round 1	Wimborne Town	6	Gillingham Town	1	
Round 1	Witham Town	1	Hoddesdon Town	2	
Round 1	Wivenhoe Town	1	Stansted	3	
Replay	Alresford Town	1	Bemerton Heath Harlequins	5	
Replay	Bourne Town	2	New Mills	2	(aet)
	New Mills won on penalties				
Replay	Causeway United	2	Loughborough University	1	
Replay	Congleton Town	5	Cheadle Town	2	
Replay	Long Buckby	5	Felixstowe & Walton United	1	
Replay	Shoreham	2	Bedfont	0	(aet)

Round 2	Arundel	4	Crowborough Athletic	0	
Round 2	Badshot Lea	2	Faversham Town	1	
Round 2	Barwell	2	Long Eaton United	0	
Round 2	Beckenham Town	2	Carterton	1	
Round 2	Bedlington Terriers	1	Spennymoor Town	5	
Round 2	Biddulph Victoria	1	Gedling Town	0	(aet)
Round 2	Bideford	0	Welton Rovers	2	
Round 2	Blaby & Whetstone Athletic	0	Boldmere St Michaels	1	
Round 2	Bootle	2	Stone Dominoes	1	
Round 2	Brimsdown Rovers	3	London Colney	2	
Round 2	Brislington	0	Poole Town	4	
Round 2	Bristol Manor Farm	2	Saltash United	1	
Round 2	Bugbrooke St Michaels	0	Leiston	4	
Round 2	Cambridge Regional College	4	Enfield 1893	1	
Round 2	Causeway United	3	Newcastle Town	2	
Round 2	Chalfont St Peter	1	Peacehaven & Telscombe	5	
Round 2	Chertsey Town	2	Croydon	0	
Round 2	Christchurch	2	Almondsbury Town	5	
Round 2	Coalville Town	4	Oadby Town	2	(aet)
Round 2	Congleton Town	0	Shildon	2	
Round 2	Crook Town	2	Bacup Borough	0	
Round 2	Daisy Hill	2	Armthorpe Welfare	3	(aet)
Round 2	Dawlish Town	3	Wimborne Town	1	
Round 2	Dunkirk	3	Lincoln Moorlands Railway	1	
Round 2	Eastbourne United	4	Hamble ASSC	2	
Round 2	Ely City	1	Woodbridge Town	1	(aet)
Ely City progressed to Round 3 after Woodbridge Town were disqualified.					
Round 2	FC Clacton	0	St Ives Town	2	
Round 2	Friar Lane & Epworth	1	Tipton Town	2	
Round 2	Glossop North End	1	Dunston UTS	0	
Round 2	Gresley	3	Ollerton Town	1	
Round 2	Herne Bay	0	Flackwell Heath	1	
Round 2	Kirkley & Pakefield	2	Biggleswade United	0	
Round 2	Long Buckby	2	Stansted	1	
Round 2	Longwell Green Sports	2	Willand Rovers	3	(aet)
Round 2	Moneyfields	2	Epsom & Ewell	3	
Round 2	Needham Market	5	Bedford	0	
Round 2	Nelson	3	Morpeth Town	1	
Round 2	New Mills	6	Tividale	1	
Round 2	Newcastle Benfield	1	Marske United	2	
Round 2	Newport Pagnell Town	3	Dereham Town	1	
Round 2	North Greenford United	0	Daventry Town	1	
Round 2	Padiham	2	Norton & Stockton Ancients	4	
Round 2	Penrith	5	Hallam	2	
Round 2	Plymouth Parkway	3	Bitton	2	
Round 2	Redhill	1	Shoreham	2	
Round 2	Scarborough Athletic	2	Bridlington Town	5	
Round 2	Shortwood United	3	Bemerton Heath Harlequins	0	
Round 2	Sleaford Town	2	Bewdley Town	1	
Round 2	Stanway Rovers	1	Hadley	0	
Round 2	Stewarts & Lloyds	2	Stotfold	4	(aet)
Round 2	Tavistock	1	Brockenhurst	3	
Round 2	Tiptree United	4	Cogenhoe United	3	(aet)
Round 2	Wellingborough Town	0	Royston Town	4	
Round 2	Wellington	3	Stratford Town	0	
Round 2	Wellington Town	3	Bradford Town	2	
Round 2	Wells City	2	Larkhall Athletic	3	(aet)

Round 2	Wembley	1	Hoddesdon Town	2	
Round 2	West Auckland Town	4	Whickham	0	
Round 2	Westfields	1	Rainworth MW	2	
Round 2	Whitehawk	3	Fareham Town	2	(aet)
Round 2	Whitley Bay	2	Alsager Town	0	
Round 2	Winsford United	1	Pickering Town	2	
Round 2	Witney United	5	Erith & Belvedere	1	
Round 2	Wroxham	0	Halstead Town	0	(aet)
Replay	Halstead Town	1	Wroxham	3	
Round 3	Armthorpe Welfare	2	Bridlington Town	1	
Round 3	Barwell	2	Glossop North End	0	
Round 3	Biddulph Victoria	1	Causeway United	3	
Round 3	Brimsdown Rovers	3	Newport Pagnell Town	2	(aet)
Round 3	Cambridge Regional College	1	Needham Market	2	
Round 3	Chertsey Town	3	Sleaford Town	2	(aet)
Round 3	Coalville Town	0	Tipton Town	2	
Round 3	Crook Town	2	Shildon	4	
Round 3	Dawlish Town	3	Brockenhurst	1	(aet)
Round 3	Eastbourne United	3	Poole Town	5	(aet)
Round 3	Flackwell Heath	1	Wroxham	3	
Round 3	Gresley	1	Spennymoor Town	0	
Round 3	Hoddesdon Town	0	Kirkley & Pakefield	4	
Round 3	Larkhall Athletic	0	Whitehawk	2	
Round 3	Leiston	3	Daventry Town	4	(aet)
Round 3	Long Buckby	5	Wellington	2	
Round 3	Marske United	5	Nelson	0	
Round 3	New Mills	5	West Auckland Town	1	
Round 3	Peacehaven & Telscombe	0	Bristol Manor Farm	3	
Round 3	Penrith	1	Bootle	4	
Round 3	Pickering Town	1	Dunkirk	1	(aet)
Round 3	Plymouth Parkway	4	Arundel	2	(aet)
Round 3	Rainworth MW	1	Norton & Stockton Ancients	2	
Round 3	Royston Town	2	Stanway Rovers	1	
Round 3	Shortwood United	2	Shoreham	0	
Round 3	St Ives Town	3	Ely City	0	
Round 3	Stotfold	3	Badshot Lea	1	
Round 3	Tiptree United	3	Beckenham Town	2	
Round 3	Wellington Town	2	Epsom & Ewell	3	(aet)
Round 3	Whitley Bay	3	Boldmere St Michaels	1	
Round 3	Willand Rovers	6	Welton Rovers	1	
Round 3	Witney United	4	Almondsbury Town	0	
Replay	Dunkirk	2	Pickering Town	2	(aet)
	Pickering Town won on penalties				
Round 4	Armthorpe Welfare	1	Wroxham	1	(aet)
Round 4	Brimsdown Rovers	1	Daventry Town	4	
Round 4	Bristol Manor Farm	1	Whitehawk	3	
Round 4	Chertsey Town	6	Plymouth Parkway	0	
Round 4	Dawlish Town	4	Gresley	4	(aet)
Round 4	Long Buckby	3	Epsom & Ewell	2	
Round 4	Needham Market	5	Kirkley & Pakefield	3	
Round 4	New Mills	2	Witney United	1	
Round 4	Norton & Stockton Ancients	4	Bootle	2	
Round 4	Pickering Town	1	Marske United	2	
Round 4	Royston Town	2	Tipton Town	1	(aet)
Round 4	Shortwood United	0	Barwell	3	

Round 4	Stotfold	0	Shildon	2	
Round 4	Tiptree United	0	St Ives Town	7	
Round 4	Whitley Bay	3	Poole Town	1	
Round 4	Willand Rovers	2	Causeway United	0	
Replay	Gresley	1	Dawlish Town	1	(aet)
	Gresley won on penalties				
Replay	Wroxham	1	Armthorpe Welfare	1	(aet)
	Wroxham won on penalties				
Round 5	Chertsey Town	1	Whitley Bay	1	(aet)
Round 5	Long Buckby	3	Gresley	4	
Round 5	Needham Market	2	Daventry Town	0	
Round 5	New Mills	0	Norton & Stockton Ancients	2	
Round 5	Royston Town	0	Wroxham	5	
Round 5	St Ives Town	1	Shildon	3	(aet)
Round 5	Whitehawk	1	Marske United	1	(aet)
Round 5	Willand Rovers	2	Barwell	2	(aet)
Replay	Barwell	2	Willand Rovers	1	(aet)
Replay	Marske United	2	Whitehawk	3	
Replay	Whitley Bay	2	Chertsey Town	1	
Round 6	Barwell	3	Norton & Stockton Ancients	0	
Round 6	Gresley	1	Whitehawk	3	
Round 6	Needham Market	1	Wroxham	2	
Round 6	Shildon	1	Whitley Bay	5	
Semi-finals					
1st leg	Barwell	3	Whitley Bay	3	
2nd leg	Whitley Bay	3	Barwell	2	
	Whitley Bay won 6-5 on aggregate				
1st leg	Whitehawk	0	Wroxham	2	
2nd leg	Wroxham	2	Whitehawk	1	
	Wroxham won 4-1 on aggregate				
FINAL	Whitley Bay	6	Wroxham	1	

Football Conference Blue Square Premier Fixtures 2010/2011 Season	AFC Wimbledon	Altrincham	Barrow	Bath City	Cambridge United	Crawley Town	Darlington	Eastbourne Borough	Fleetwood Town	Forest Green Rovers	Gateshead	Grimsby Town	Hayes & Yeading	Histon	Kettering Town	Kidderminster Harriers	Luton Town	Mansfield Town	Newport County	Rushden & Diamonds	Southport	Tamworth	Wrexham	York City
AFC Wimbledon		26/02	02/04	11/09	28/09	21/09	30/10	28/12	05/02	02/10	16/10	30/04	01/01	17/08	20/11	12/03	30/11	23/04	30/08	26/03	22/01	21/08	18/12	12/02
Altrincham	09/11		21/09	22/01	02/04	21/08	17/08	30/04	16/10	30/11	05/03	25/09	25/01	18/12	19/02	04/09	13/11	30/08	23/04	02/10	05/02	19/03	01/01	28/12
Barrow	13/11	29/01		26/03	08/01	09/10	30/08	11/09	28/09	18/09	17/08	23/04	30/04	25/01	09/04	27/11	02/10	19/02	09/11	21/08	01/01	18/12	28/12	05/03
Bath City	25/01	05/10	04/09		29/01	30/11	18/09	09/10	20/11	28/12	02/04	19/03	09/11	23/04	05/03	28/09	08/01	30/04	01/01	17/08	18/12	12/02	30/08	21/08
Cambridge United	09/04	27/11	16/10	02/10		17/08	18/12	30/08	30/04	26/03	04/09	09/11	23/04	01/01	21/09	19/02	26/02	28/12	25/09	05/02	21/08	20/11	22/01	19/03
Crawley Town	19/03	20/11	26/02	24/08	25/01		02/04	01/01	04/09	30/08	18/09	14/08	28/12	05/03	08/01	02/10	29/01	18/12	16/10	23/04	27/11	28/09	12/02	30/04
Darlington	08/01	26/03	03/01	09/04	05/03	13/11		12/02	26/12	11/09	28/08	24/08	09/10	30/11	29/01	04/12	21/09	25/01	14/08	30/04	25/09	09/11	02/10	23/04
Eastbourne Borough	28/08	18/09	19/03	25/04	03/01	26/12	04/09		09/04	09/11	04/12	29/01	17/08	19/02	26/03	16/04	16/10	08/01	13/11	28/09	05/03	27/11	21/08	02/10
Fleetwood Town	27/11	16/04	25/04	25/09	09/10	12/03	01/01	26/02		29/01	09/11	19/02	22/01	02/10	11/09	21/09	21/08	17/08	18/12	13/11	28/12	02/04	19/03	30/08
Forest Green Rovers	25/04	09/04	12/03	28/08	16/04	03/01	19/02	21/09	08/01		21/08	05/10	05/02	16/10	25/09	26/12	04/12	13/11	19/03	27/11	04/09	26/02	17/08	30/10
Gateshead	29/01	11/09	30/11	26/02	30/10	26/03	28/12	12/03	24/08	20/11		21/09	18/12	09/04	14/08	08/01	25/09	02/10	30/04	12/02	07/09	09/10	23/04	01/01
Grimsby Town	05/03	25/04	20/11	16/04	12/02	22/01	26/02	30/10	18/09	18/12	05/02		21/08	30/08	30/11	09/04	04/09	01/01	02/10	28/12	16/10	26/03	28/09	17/08
Hayes & Yeading	26/12	30/10	25/09	14/08	05/10	28/08	16/04	30/11	26/03	24/08	19/03	13/11		04/09	25/04	29/01	03/01	09/04	21/09	04/12	19/02	08/01	16/10	26/02
Histon	16/04	09/10	14/08	27/11	26/12	11/09	12/03	24/08	04/12	02/04	28/09	03/01	12/02		28/08	13/11	25/04	19/03	29/01	26/02	05/10	18/09	30/10	08/01
Kettering Town	04/09	28/09	12/02	04/12	13/11	05/02	21/08	22/01	25/01	23/04	27/11	12/03	02/10	28/12		16/10	17/08	09/11	26/02	30/08	30/04	01/01	18/09	02/04
Kidderminster Harr.	25/09	12/02	22/01	05/02	18/09	08/03	19/03	20/11	23/04	01/01	05/10	09/10	11/09	30/04	18/12		02/04	21/08	28/12	09/11	17/08	30/08	26/02	30/11
Luton Town	18/09	14/08	05/02	30/10	11/09	05/10	27/11	23/04	12/02	09/10	22/01	25/01	30/08	20/11	19/03	05/03		28/09	24/08	01/01	09/04	28/12	30/04	18/12
Mansfield Town	05/10	03/01	04/12	12/03	28/08	30/10	16/10	25/09	30/11	14/08	25/04	26/12	20/11	22/01	24/08	26/03	16/04		12/02	02/04	26/02	04/09	29/01	21/09
Newport County	03/01	12/03	16/04	26/12	04/12	25/04	05/02	05/10	05/03	28/09	29/03	02/04	27/11	21/08	30/10	28/08	19/02	18/09		22/01	20/11	17/08	04/09	09/10
Rushden & Diams.	24/08	08/01	30/10	19/02	30/11	25/09	05/10	18/12	14/08	08/03	16/04	28/08	05/03	21/09	03/01	25/04	26/12	09/10	11/09		19/03	29/01	09/04	20/11
Southport	14/08	24/08	26/12	13/11	12/03	16/04	25/04	02/04	28/08	12/02	03/01	04/12	28/09	01/03	09/10	30/10	26/03	11/09	08/01	18/09		02/10	30/11	29/01
Tamworth	19/02	04/12	05/10	21/09	24/08	09/04	22/01	14/08	30/10	30/04	13/11	11/09	12/03	05/02	26/12	03/01	28/08	05/03	30/11	16/10	23/04		29/03	25/09
Wrexham	09/10	26/12	28/8	03/01	14/08	04/12	20/11	05/02	05/10	05/03	19/02	08/01	02/04	25/09	16/04	24/08	09/11	27/11	26/03	12/03	21/09	25/04		11/09
York City	04/12	28/08	24/08	16/10	25/04	19/02	28/09	29/03	03/01	22/01	26/12	27/11	18/09	26/03	05/10	14/08	12/03	05/02	09/04	04/09	09/11	16/04	13/11	

Please note that the above fixtures may be subject to change.

Football Conference Blue Square North Fixtures 2010/2011 Season

	AFC Telford United	Alfreton Town	Blyth Spartans	Boston United	Corby Town	Droylsden	Eastwood Town	Gainsborough Trinity	Gloucester City	Guiseley	Harrogate Town	Hinckley United	Hyde United	Ilkeston Town	Nuneaton Town	Redditch United	Solihull Moors	Stafford Rangers	Stalybridge Celtic	Vauxhall Motors	Worcester City	Workington
AFC Telford United	■	22/02	04/09	09/04	26/02	15/01	18/12	05/02	24/08	27/11	30/04	22/01	14/08	12/03	30/08	28/12	06/11	01/01	26/03	23/04	02/10	23/10
Alfreton Town	16/10	■	28/12	18/09	12/03	02/04	01/01	24/08	18/12	26/02	13/11	14/08	26/03	29/01	30/04	23/04	19/02	30/08	08/01	04/09	30/10	30/11
Blyth Spartans	04/12	28/08	■	06/11	21/08	03/01	12/02	29/03	09/04	25/04	09/11	19/02	23/10	16/04	19/03	15/01	05/03	29/01	17/08	18/09	11/09	26/12
Boston United	12/02	05/02	23/04	■	09/11	05/03	30/08	01/01	12/03	22/01	28/12	30/11	18/12	30/10	24/08	27/11	15/01	14/08	16/10	25/04	02/04	11/09
Corby Town	18/09	27/11	30/10	04/09	■	18/12	29/01	16/10	28/12	08/01	14/08	30/08	30/04	02/04	01/01	25/08	19/03	23/04	19/02	23/03	05/03	13/11
Droylsden	08/11	19/03	30/08	13/11	09/04	■	14/08	26/02	30/04	29/01	23/04	28/12	23/08	18/09	12/02	16/10	07/03	04/09	04/12	01/01	08/01	30/10
Eastwood Town	02/04	26/12	16/10	03/01	28/08	22/01	■	09/11	11/09	30/10	08/01	18/09	19/02	04/12	05/03	12/03	25/04	26/03	16/04	05/02	17/08	21/08
Gainsborough Trinity	21/08	25/04	27/11	26/12	16/04	11/09	02/10	■	15/01	17/08	12/02	19/03	02/04	03/01	18/12	06/11	22/01	19/02	05/03	23/10	26/03	28/08
Gloucester City	25/04	16/04	13/11	08/01	17/08	02/10	26/02	30/10	■	18/09	16/10	05/02	04/09	21/08	02/04	30/08	03/01	19/03	01/02	27/11	26/12	22/01
Guiseley	05/03	15/01	24/08	23/10	02/10	06/11	30/04	23/04	19/02	■	01/01	04/12	30/08	23/11	14/08	04/09	02/04	18/12	13/11	28/12	12/03	05/02
Harrogate Town	19/02	04/12	05/02	28/08	06/11	17/08	23/10	12/03	26/03	26/12	■	04/09	02/10	22/01	15/01	26/02	21/08	27/11	03/01	09/04	16/04	25/04
Hinckley United	16/04	06/11	02/04	16/08	03/01	28/08	15/01	29/01	08/11	11/09	18/12	■	27/11	26/12	26/02	26/03	23/10	02/10	21/08	12/02	25/04	05/03
Hyde United	29/01	21/08	22/01	16/04	11/09	25/04	25/10	13/11	12/02	03/01	19/03	09/04	■	28/08	06/11	18/09	04/12	08/01	26/12	26/02	16/10	16/08
Ilkeston Town	13/11	23/10	18/12	19/03	05/02	26/03	04/11	30/08	06/11	12/02	05/03	01/01	28/12	■	23/04	30/04	02/10	24/08	09/04	14/08	27/11	15/01
Nuneaton Town	03/01	11/09	08/01	25/04	26/12	21/08	13/11	09/04	04/12	26/03	18/09	30/10	25/01	17/08	■	29/01	09/11	16/10	28/08	12/03	19/02	16/04
Redditch United	28/08	17/08	02/10	21/08	25/04	19/02	09/04	04/12	05/03	16/04	30/10	08/01	05/02	11/09	23/10	■	26/12	01/03	22/01	13/11	03/01	19/03
Solihull Moors	11/09	09/04	14/08	26/03	12/02	27/11	24/08	30/04	28/08	16/10	29/01	23/04	12/03	08/01	28/12	01/01	■	30/10	18/09	18/12	13/11	26/02
Stafford Rangers	26/12	03/01	12/03	26/02	22/01	16/04	06/11	18/09	23/10	21/08	02/04	13/11	05/03	25/04	05/02	12/02	17/08	■	11/09	15/01	28/08	04/12
Stalybridge Celtic	30/10	02/10	26/02	29/01	15/01	23/10	28/12	04/09	23/04	19/03	30/08	12/03	01/01	09/11	27/11	14/08	05/02	30/04	■	24/08	18/12	02/04
Vauxhall Motors	17/08	05/03	26/03	02/10	04/12	26/12	19/03	08/01	29/01	28/08	11/09	16/10	30/10	19/02	22/01	02/04	16/04	09/11	25/04	■	21/08	03/01
Worcester City	19/03	22/01	30/04	04/12	23/10	05/02	23/04	14/08	01/01	09/04	29/11	23/08	15/01	26/02	04/09	08/11	30/08	28/12	12/02	06/11	■	18/09
Workington	08/01	12/02	01/01	19/02	26/03	12/03	27/11	28/12	14/08	09/11	24/08	30/04	23/04	16/10	02/10	18/12	04/09	09/04	06/11	30/08	29/01	■

Please note that the above fixtures may be subject to change.

Football Conference Blue Square South Fixtures 2010/2011 Season	Basingstoke Town	Bishop's Stortford	Boreham Wood	Braintree Town	Bromley	Chelmsford City	Dartford	Dorchester Town	Dover Athletic	Eastleigh	Ebbsfleet United	Farnborough	Hampton & Richmond Borough	Havant & Waterlooville	Lewes	Maidenhead United	St. Albans City	Staines Town	Thurrock	Welling United	Weston-super-Mare	Woking
Basingstoke Town		13/11	25/04	04/09	16/10	14/08	12/03	23/08	05/02	12/02	02/04	28/08	16/04	26/03	05/03	26/12	22/01	04/12	18/09	30/10	03/01	08/01
Bishop's Stortford	09/04		08/01	01/01	30/08	22/03	29/01	30/04	30/10	12/03	21/08	04/09	18/09	16/10	09/11	27/11	23/04	17/08	28/12	05/03	04/12	12/02
Boreham Wood	19/03	11/09		26/02	17/08	15/01	02/10	12/02	13/11	23/04	16/10	29/03	06/11	09/04	30/04	29/01	01/01	28/12	21/08	18/12	27/11	30/08
Braintree Town	18/12	26/12	24/08		13/11	28/08	12/02	02/04	11/09	18/09	03/01	14/08	22/01	16/04	15/01	26/03	19/03	05/03	16/10	25/04	30/10	29/01
Bromley	15/01	03/01	12/03	09/04		27/11	23/04	14/08	26/12	30/04	02/10	06/11	26/03	24/08	23/10	18/12	11/09	12/02	26/02	28/08	29/01	09/11
Chelmsford City	06/11	22/01	08/11	28/12	25/04		30/08	04/09	19/02	21/08	26/02	16/04	04/12	05/02	12/03	02/10	23/10	09/04	01/01	26/03	08/01	16/08
Dartford	23/09	24/08	16/04	04/12	18/09	03/01		13/11	25/04	15/03	28/08	22/01	19/02	14/08	26/03	05/03	05/02	06/11	08/01	26/12	04/09	09/04
Dorchester Town	27/11	06/11	18/09	23/10	19/02	18/12	15/01		16/04	17/08	11/09	25/04	03/01	28/08	09/04	09/11	15/03	26/03	05/03	29/01	26/12	21/08
Dover Athletic	23/04	02/04	26/03	08/01	01/01	16/10	09/11	19/03		04/09	29/01	18/09	05/03	27/11	28/12	06/11	30/04	21/08	30/08	17/08	12/02	04/12
Eastleigh	02/10	14/08	30/10	19/02	05/02	05/03	16/10	22/01	18/12		16/04	26/12	25/04	03/01	11/09	23/08	15/01	13/11	09/04	19/03	28/08	26/03
Ebbsfleet United	19/02	26/03	05/03	30/08	22/01	23/04	28/12	08/01	24/08	06/11		05/02	23/10	12/03	01/01	14/08	09/04	04/09	04/12	09/11	18/09	30/04
Farnborough	28/12	18/12	23/10	12/03	02/04	30/10	21/08	26/02	15/01	01/01	18/08		13/11	29/01	02/10	11/09	19/02	30/08	30/04	27/11	26/03	23/04
Hampton & Richmond	29/01	26/02	02/04	23/04	21/08	30/04	17/08	30/08	02/10	09/11	27/11	16/10		11/09	18/12	15/01	28/12	01/01	19/03	12/02	12/03	30/10
Havant & Waterlooville	08/11	19/03	22/01	06/11	05/03	02/04	26/02	28/12	23/10	30/08	12/02	04/12	08/01		23/04	01/02	18/09	30/04	04/09	21/08	16/08	01/01
Lewes	21/08	25/04	05/02	23/03	04/12	18/09	30/10	16/10	28/08	08/01	26/12	19/03	04/09	19/02		02/04	13/11	01/01	18/08	03/01	16/04	26/02
Maidenhead United	01/01	05/02	04/12	17/08	04/09	19/03	30/04	23/04	12/03	26/02	13/11	08/01	09/04	30/10	12/02		30/08	18/09	22/01	16/10	21/08	28/12
St. Albans City	17/08	02/10	26/12	21/08	08/01	12/02	02/04	04/12	26/02	27/11	30/10	09/11	28/08	25/04	29/01	03/01		12/03	26/03	16/04	16/10	04/09
Staines Town	26/02	15/01	28/08	27/11	16/04	29/01	19/03	30/10	22/03	02/04	18/12	03/01	26/12	02/10	14/08	25/04	24/08		05/02	11/09	09/11	16/10
Thurrock	30/11	28/08	19/02	09/11	30/10	26/12	11/09	02/10	03/01	29/01	25/04	12/02	24/08	18/12	27/11	16/04	14/08	23/10		15/01	02/04	12/03
Welling United	30/04	23/10	04/09	05/02	28/12	24/08	01/01	12/03	22/01	04/12	22/03	09/04	14/08	13/11	30/08	19/02	06/11	08/01	23/04		26/02	18/09
Weston-super-Mare	30/08	19/02	14/08	30/04	30/11	11/09	18/12	01/01	09/04	28/12	19/03	23/08	05/02	15/01	06/11	23/10	05/03	23/04	13/11	02/10		22/01
Woking	11/09	16/04	03/01	02/10	19/03	13/11	27/11	05/02	14/08	23/10	15/01	05/03	15/03	26/12	24/08	28/08	18/12	19/02	06/11	02/04	25/04	

Please note that the above fixtures may be subject to change.